HAPPINESS · SUCCESS · ROMANCE · GOOD FORTUNE · ARE YOU READY FOR YOUR STAR-STUDDED FUTURE?

Whatever you desire can be yours if you just reach out to the stars for guidance. Let Sydney Omarr's unique astrological expertise show you the promise that 1984 holds in store for you with this specially charted, day-by-day horoscope for your sun sign.

With the help of the zodiac you can learn how to make the right decisions at the right time, and you'll be able to put all your assets to work for you every day of the week and every week of the year.

SYDNEY OMARR'S

Day-by-Day Astrological Guide for

CAPRICORN

(December 22–January 19)

1984

A SIGNET BOOK

NEW AMERICAN LIBRARY

TIMES MIRROR

SIGNET TRADEMARK REG. U.S. PAT. OFF. AND FOREIGN COUNTRIES
REGISTERED TRADEMARK—MARCA REGISTRADA
HECHO EN CHICAGO, U.S.A.

SIGNET, SIGNET CLASSICS, MENTOR, PLUME, MERIDIAN and NAL BOOKS
are published by The New American Library, Inc.,
1633 Broadway, New York, New York 10019

First Printing, July, 1983

1 2 3 4 5 6 7 8 9

PRINTED IN THE UNITED STATES OF AMERICA

CONTENTS

INTRODUCTION

Have you ever marveled at the fact that no two human beings are exactly alike? Have you ever been struck by the wide disparity that often exists in both looks and temperament among members of the same family unit? One of the most stunning facts of life is that each of us is a separate, distinct individual—a first-time phenomenon in the history of the world. Human diversity is one of the world's greatest wonders . . . and one of life's greatest potential problems.

Because we are so different, no one yet has been able to devise one simple, fail-safe system for finding success and happiness. Each of us has to find the way through his or her own personal maze, with very few reliable road signs. Here and there we may come upon some crumbs of experience dropped by an older and wiser Hansel or Gretel; but, in the main, we're on our own to tap-dance our way around the innumerable pitfalls each day reveals.

If there is a secret for finding the right path to personal fulfillment, it appears to be self-knowledge. People of great wisdom have been telling us so for eons, and our most time-honored role models tend to be those who dared to plumb their personal depths. Today, self-understanding is the goal of most therapies, from psychoanalysis to hypnotic regression. In effect, these methods say that if we know why we feel, think, and act as we do, we can be in much better control of our lives and destinies. This concept is the theory, and self-understanding is the goal, of contemporary astrology as well.

Modern astrologers know that the horoscope—one's individual astrological imprint—stands alongside other factors such as genetics and early environment in accounting for personal uniqueness. Many astrologers now combine study of their ancient craft with investigation of biological and social sciences, particularly human psychology. There is also a heightened awareness that astrology really was and is a tool for probing the mystery of the human psyche. While shunning the sterile, empty conclusions of the behaviorists, astrologers do in general adhere to the theory that we create what happens to us by how we happen to the world. It is the *why* of our actions that is the key to our destiny.

Then what is the "magic" of the magic wheel of the horoscope? What do astrologers know that is hidden from the rest of us? Quite literally, the astrologer's special talent is fluency in the most ancient language in our solar system—the language of the movements of the sun, moon, and planets in the sky above us, movements observed since the beginning of intelligent life on earth, spoken of since the beginning of oral tradition, recorded since the beginning of written history. By translating this language, astrologers provide us with a wealth of "inside information." Operating on the principle that what goes on above is mirrored in our world below, they crack the celestial code ... giving us extraordinary insights into human behavior, and alerting us to the probable influences on that behavior as the world turns.

The most basic thing astrologers do is to classify people according to their temperaments. The broadest division is by "sun sign"—twelve different ways human beings have been observed to perceive and react to the

2

world. Your sun sign, determined by what segment of the zodiac the sun was moving through during the month you were born, stamps you with the set of characteristics—both "good" and "bad"—that are most easily available to you, though you can choose among them. For instance, Leo's legendary desire to be at the center of things can manifest itself as mere vanity and showiness—or as true leadership ability.

In the main this book deals with your sun sign, because it is the one astrological fact most people know about themselves. Your total "horoscope" (see next section) is much more complex and must be calculated individually. However, your sun sign is still your horoscope's foundation, in terms both of your character and of the probable crossroads you will come to as you go along from day to day.

With that in mind, use this book as a "planning guide" for the year to come. Heed what it has to say about both your potential assets and your avoidable liabilities; check out your compatibility with other astrological personalities; see how you can look for love in the right places; find out which career areas are most likely to yield personal success and fulfillment; learn what time it is for you according to the great celestial clock. And—perhaps most important—use the inside information the daily forecasts give you to plan your moves with precision. It's more than a truism that life is timing, and knowing when to act is often the key to everything.

1. TEST YOUR A.Q. (ASTROLOGY QUOTIENT)

Astrology is enjoying a new vigor as contemporary interest in the ancient subject grows, both in width and in depth. There is a positive awareness that far from being a "new-age" fad, astrology has a long and fascinating past, as well as an active and stimulating present. If you are one of the many people who pride themselves on being "astrology-smart," you can find out just how good a handle you have on the subject by checking your knowledge against the quiz on the next few pages. The questions are those most asked by both the average person and the beginning astrologer; the answers are designed not only to provide information, but also to lay to rest some popular misconceptions.

As the earth gradually slips into the Age of Aquarius, there is an increased openness to "occult" knowledge. One benchmark: There are surprising numbers of people today who know that the word "occult" simply means "hidden" or obscured from view. As astrology discards some of its wrappings, it will also leave behind a great deal of its mystery. Most astrologers welcome the fact that a little light is being shed on their chosen profession, because they are anxious to bring it into the modern world. However, there is another good reason for "opening up" astrology, and that is its incredible richness as a subject of study.

To enter the world of astrology is to encounter myth,

symbol, language, literature, theology, psychology, metaphysics, and philosophy—not to mention science and mathematics. It's unlikely you will ever become an astrologer, or penetrate much below the surface of the subject. However, with the mini-course in these pages, you can increase your A.Q. at least tenfold—and be light years ahead of most people.

How old is astrology?

There are traditions in many parts of the world, including India and China, that as early as 3000 to 2000 B.C. men were observing the heavens and calculating the movement of the planets, which were thought to be gods. Credit for developing an astrological system more or less as we know it is generally given to the astrologer-priests of the Chaldeans in Mesopotamia, starting about 700 B.C. It is from that time that we have actual records of observations of how movements of the bodies in the sky corresponded to events on earth. The Romans picked up on astrology, which they learned from the Greeks, about 300 B.C. However, in Rome astrologers had to compete with other types of soothsayers plying their predictive trades. Astrology remained synonymous with astronomy and to some extent theology until many centuries later when astrology became more "personalized." During the Renaissance, astrology experienced a heyday, though certain factions in the church condemned it for being "fatalistic." In the fourteenth and fifteenth centuries, if you were anybody, you had your own personal astrologer. The so-called Age of Enlightenment or scientific era (c. 1600) dealt a pretty heavy blow to astrology, from which it did not begin to recover until the mid to late 1800s. Today, astrology is alive and well, and is beginning to make its peace with some scientifically minded skeptics.

What is the difference between astrology and astronomy?

At one time there was no difference. All astrologers were astronomers (and vice versa) and were accorded a great deal of prestige. With the dawn of the scientific era some two hundred years ago there came a split between the two disciplines, and they went their separate ways. Now the astronomer measures and calculates planetary positions, and the astrologer interprets the data in terms of human life. One of the best statements of the relationship between the two pursuits was made by Ralph Waldo Emerson: "Astrology is astronomy brought to earth and applied to the affairs of men."

What is the zodiac?

The word "zodiac" literally means "circle of animals" and probably was originally used to refer to the constellations, which supplied the names for the twelve signs. For many centuries the word has *not* referred to the constellations, but to an imaginary 360-degree band around the earth which begins at the point where the sun reaches zero degrees, Aries (the vernal equinox and the beginning of the agricultural year). The signs follow each other at 30-degree intervals along the board until the sun reaches 29 degrees of Pisces, the last day of winter. Points along the zodiac are the astrologer's frame of reference, as well as the celestial navigator's.

Why do we say the sun has "moved" into a sign when we know the sun doesn't move?

There is evidence that even the earliest astrologers were aware that the sun is the center of our solar system and that the earth as well as the other planets orbit around it. (One of the gems of ancient knowledge which went into obscurity during the dark ages of man.) We say the sun "moves" because astrology is an observed science which deals with the *apparent* movement of the heavenly bodies from our reference point here on earth. The apparent path of the sun as it "moves" through the signs throughout the year is actually the path of the earth as it orbits the sun. We all use similar terminology when we speak of the sun "coming up" and "going down."

What is a horoscope?

The word "horoscope," which comes from the Greek, literally means "watcher of the hour." As the word is used today, your horoscope is the map an astrologer draws of the positions of the sun and the planets in the heavens at the moment you were born. It is often referred to as your birth chart or natal chart. The word "horoscope" is often loosely used to mean your forecast or prediction for the day, week, or year.

How does an astrologer draw up a chart or horoscope?

The astrologer's basic tool is an ephemeris—an astronomically calculated reference book which gives the exact positions of the sun and the planets with relation to the 360-degree circle of the zodiac for every day of any given year. Using the ephemeris, as well as other reference books such as an atlas, the astrologer computes the positions of the planets exactly, and draws a precise picture of the sky as if he were standing at your birthplace at the moment you took your first breath. The more important work of the astrologer is his *interpretation* of your chart—a complex process requiring much skill and training.

Why is it important to the astrologer to know the time of day you were born?

A horoscope is like a great wheel or pie divided into twelve segments called "houses." Each house indicates a particular sphere of human experience—the self, others,

8

children, work, career, romance, marriage, etc. Within any given twenty-four-hour period, the wheel makes a full cycle, and so boundaries of the house change from minute to minute. What your time of birth tells the astrologer is which houses of the horoscope the planets of your chart fall into—an extremely important factor in determining the action of the planets for you individually. The placement of the sun in the houses is particularly significant, as the sun is "you" in essence—the conscious self. If you know your time of birth within an hour or so, you can find out which "house" is your sun's "home" in a later chapter of this book. In most states, birth times are on record going back quite a number of years. There is generally a Bureau of Vital Statistics which can tell you this information about your birth.

What is most important in astrology—the planets, the signs of the zodiac, or the houses?

All three are about equal in importance when spelling out character or events, but each has a different function. There is a theatrical metaphor that helps to clarify them. Think of the planet as the actor, the sign as the costume and makeup the actor wears, and the house as the particular set against which the action is staged. It is then easier to see that the planet provides the actual action or "event," that the sign the planet is in gives the action its particular color and meaning, and that the house suggests which area of life is being affected.

What does it mean to be "born on the cusp"?

If your birthday falls either at the very beginning or very end of a sign, you are said to be "born on the cusp"—the dividing line between two signs. Contrary to popular belief, "cusp" days vary from year to year, and signs do not always begin or end on the same date (or time). If you are unsure about your birth sign, use the tables on pages 61 to 67, which give the exact day and hour the sun changed signs every month of every year from 1910 to 1975. Though astrologers differ on the subject, the general consensus is that an individual is influenced by only *one* sun sign, no matter how close the call.

Does astrology work? How does it work?

Most people are not satisfied with the answer that astrology works because—on the empirical evidence of thousands of years—it *works*. They quite naturally want more evidence. The advent of the computer has spurred a great many elaborate research projects which may eventually supply enough data to convince some of the skeptical. The more interesting question is *how* astrology works. Within the astrological community there are a number of different schools of thought on the subject, but the prevailing theories tend to be metaphysical rather than strictly scientific. One is that at the moment of our first breath as we take our place in the universe we are "imprinted" with a pattern—the pattern of placement of the sun, moon, and planets in the various zodiacal signs and their relationship to each other at that moment. The imprint becomes both our individual personality and the "road map" for our lives on earth (which can indicate a number of different routes). Few astrologers believe that specific events are foreordained by this planetary pattern; rather, it affects our character and personality which are the key to our actions— and hence our destinies. However, no horoscope indicates unlimited possibilities for the individual. Within the parameters of our given talents and temperament, we are free to make our own decisions. One of the purposes of astrological predictions, such as those found in this book, is to alert the individuals born under a certain sun sign to the influence and possibilities that are in effect at a given time. What actually happens depends on how we react.

Is there any evidence that the planets really influence us?

The first and most obvious evidence that at least one "planet" has a measurable effect on earth's affairs is the influence of the moon. Even schoolchildren know that the gravitational pull of the moon controls the tides; modern research indicates that the moon has a much wider range of measurable effects. For instance, experiments show that cycles of the moon dictate the daily, and often yearly, rhythms of many life forms, including the oyster. No woman will argue that she does not experience a cycle virtually identical with that of the moon. Increasingly doctors schedule surgery away from the time of the full moon because blood has been observed to flow more freely at that time. It is also well documented that hospitals and emergency clinics find an upsurge in mentally distressed people at this critical time of the month. However, it requires a huge mental leap from the moon's evidence to a conclusion that the other planets affect us in some "scientific" or clearly explainable way. One theory is that electromagnetic emanations from the other planets interact with our body chemistry in a way similar to the gravitational pull of the moon—but it remains theory.

Doesn't the discovery of "new" planets change things from an astrological point of view?

Earliest records tell us that astrologer-astronomers have always been aware of seven "planets": the sun (which is actually a star), the moon (which is a satellite of earth), Mercury, Venus, Mars, Jupiter, and Saturn. That lineup did not change until 1781, when Uranus was discovered; then came the discoveries, much later, of Neptune and Pluto. The revelations of these "modern" planets serve to extend astrologers' knowledge rather than to refute it. With the technological ability to compute the positions of Uranus, Neptune, and Pluto at any point in history, astrologers are able to check out their effects on people and events, and actually see new "reasons" for certain phenomena.

Are astrologers psychic?

Some may be, but psychic or extrasensory powers are not required to become an astrologer. The astrologer bases his interpretation of your personality and his predictions for your future on both historical observations and his own perceptions. As they study and practice, astrologers build up their own bank of information about how certain patterns in the horoscope manifest themselves in the lives and the personalities of people. If the astrologer appears to be "psychic" it is usually because he has sharpened his skills to a very high point. An important theory to remember if you visit an astrologer is that astrology is *not* meant to be a guessing game. To give the most helpful and constructive reading, the astrologer has to know certain pertinent facts about your past and present: whether you are married or single, whether you have children, what you do for a living, and so on. The most obvious reason for supplying this kind of data is to let the astrologer know what *is* happening so he can help you figure out how you might change things, on the basis of the influences he sees coming up in your chart.

How can I find an astrologer/study astrology/become an astrologer?

These three questions often run together as a person first becomes conscious of the tremendous value and validity of astrology to our modern lives. The first question is most easily answered. There are several organizations in the United States for practicing astrologers: the American Federation of Astrologers (P.O. Box 22040, Tempe, AZ 85282), the National Astrological Society (Box 75, Old Chelsea Station, New York, NY 10011), and the National Council for Geocosmic Research (200 West 20th Street, New York, NY 10011), to name the most well known. By writing to one of these associations you can get the names of astrologers practicing in your area. At this point there is no certificate or license needed to practice astrology, and astrological competence does vary. Word-of-mouth reference is often the best way to find one. Although there is no substitute for experience, there are any number of gifted young astrologers who are bringing new insights to this ancient art.

If you would like to study astrology, you might find out the names of schools and/or individual instructors near you by inquiring through the same associations, or by checking your local telephone directory. (Unlike "fortune-tellers," astrologers are permitted to advertise in certain states and communities.) As for becoming an astrologer, think long and hard before you take the plunge into serious study. Astrology is a very demanding, highly complex discipline which requires years of dedicated work. It is one subject where a little knowledge can truly be a dangerous thing. The modern astrologer is a kind of counselor, and while there is a strict code of ethics legitimate astrologers adhere to, it is easy for the novice to give the wrong "advice."

What is the Age of Aquarius?

In recent years the so-called "Age of Aquarius" has gotten a lot of press—and some mixed reviews. Here's what astrologers mean when they use the phrase.

13

From our reference point on earth, the vernal equinox (beginning of the zodiac and the seasonal year) appears to "slip backward" year after year—a fact astronomers attribute to the wobble of the earth as it rotates on its axis. For the past two thousand years or so, the zero point has been in the sign of Pisces, but sometime soon it should be entering the sign of Aquarius, where it will be for the next two thousand years: the Age of Aquarius. To astrologers, each twenty-century period is known as a "great age," and each age has been observed to correspond to a different set of historical/sociological conditions here on earth. The exact year when the Age of Pisces ends and the age of Aquarius begins is a matter of dispute. Judging by such revolutionary movements as equal rights and women's liberation (typical of Uranus-ruled Aquarius), some astrologers believe we have already entered the new age. Others say we are in a period of transition, and that these movements are "early warnings" of the tremendous social and cultural changes to come. Some things that can be said to typify the Age of Aquarius are group consciousness, radical technological advances, the equalizing of all members of society, a feeling of brotherhood, and an emphasis on reason rather than faith. This last is one major point of difference between the new age and the age of Pisces, which corresponds with the Christian era.

Are there different kinds of astrology?

Astrology as we know it grows out of western tradition, and differs in a number of ways from the astrology practiced in India and China. Even within "western" astrology there are a number of schools of thought, but their differences are too subtle and complex to be of interest to the beginner. What is useful to know is that there are different branches within the western astrology that is generally practiced here.

When an astrologer does your horoscope, he is practicing "natal" astrology—which deals with your moment of birth, and how the pattern of the planets affects your growth and development as a human being. Natal astrology can deal with the birth of anything, from a person to a company to a country.

An astrologer might also practice "mundane" astrology, which deals with affairs of state, world politics, and social and economic conditions. When asked to answer a specific question about the probable outcome of any matter, the astrologer might employ the "horary" technique. "Horary" means hour, so a chart is set up for the moment the question is asked. The astrologer divines the answer by interpreting the message of that chart. The principle of "asking the cosmos" at a particular point in time also underlies the *I Ching* and Tarot card readings. "Electional" astrology is a variation on this theme. If you want to know when is the right time to get married, start a business, ask for a raise, have a baby, etc., the astrologer will use a trial-and-error technique to arrive at the right date and time for you. Electional astrology is related to locational astrology, which can theoretically tell you the best choice of geographic location for you or your project.

Within "natal" astrology, the branch most of us are familiar with and will find most pertinent, there are also a couple of subdivisions. "Synastry," which literally means "stars together," is the art of comparing the birth charts of two people to ascertain the nature of the relationship and how it is likely to work in the long run. Many people consult astrologers for synastry charts before they marry. Medical astrology also has a long and prestigious history. The birth or natal chart is a diagnostic tool for practitioners of this art, who can

15

pinpoint or anticipate specific health problems from it. In the strong words of Hippocrates, who is generally regarded as the father of medicine and whose ethical theories guide physicians even today: "He who does not understand astrology is not a doctor but fool." The branch of natal astrology that deals with our immortal rather than temporal lives is called "esoteric" astrology. The birth chart is regarded as a guide to spiritual evolution, and there is usually a strong emphasis on both Christian theology and such oriental ideas as reincarnation and "karma"—a doctrine which explains good and evil in terms of the carryover we bear from previous lifetimes.

2. WHY A SIGN?—THE ELEMENTS AND QUALITIES

There's one aspect of astrology most people agree upon: It's fun. Human beings love to "type" other human beings, and astrology offers a neat and benign system—benign because it allows us to point out other people's foibles without attributing them to sex, race, religion, country of origin, or any other factor that might imply prejudice. Astrology is completely fair: You're overly emotional because you're a Cancer, not because you're the youngest child; you're stubborn and pigheaded because you're a Taurus, not because of where your parents came from; you're an oversexed home-wrecker because you're a Scorpio, not because you totally lack self-control. By the same token, we can flatter ourselves by assuming we possess the better characteristics of our own sun sign: "I'm a Libra, so naturally I must be sweet and pleasant all the time"; "I couldn't have made that mistake, because I'm a careful and conscientious Virgo"; "My Sagittarian sun may make me sloppy, but it gives me energy to burn." When someone poses the question "What is the best sign in the Zodiac?" you can bet that the expected answer is the one the question poser was born under.

But even allowing for such harmless distortions, "what's my sign" is an amazingly easy game to play, and most people can become rather good at it. What's missing in parlor-game astrology is the "why" of the signs, which is essential to really understanding them.

A Sign Is a Symbol

The twelve signs of the zodiac are associated with twelve different representative "pictures"—most of them animal, like the Aries ram, Taurus bull, and Leo lion; some of them human, like the Aquarian water-bearer and Gemini twins; one, the Sagittarian Centaur, half man half animal; and one inanimate—the scales of Libra. Each sign also has a "glyph" or shorthand marking that is used to designate it, such as the familiar horns of the ram. Are we to take these pictures literally and describe the signs in terms of such limited parameters as animal behavior? No. A zodiac sign is a symbol, and like all symbols, it stands for a complex idea not easily expressed in words—certainly not a few words. Think of the cross, one of our most powerful symbols, and the richness of associations it carries with it. The swastika is another example; contrast it with our familiar symbol of the American flag. Some symbols, such as the swastika and American flag, cause different responses in different people. Not so with the signs; they form a symbol system that is mutually agreed upon and has been for centuries. And each sign-symbol carries a wealth of history, tradition, and meaning.

Just as modern science tends to support the view that there is nothing random in the universe, astrologers know there is nothing arbitrary about the designations of certain characteristics to each of the zodiac sign-symbols. Underlying everything there is a beautifully integrated and perfectly logical system of interlocking parts: the elements and the qualities.

Why Twelve Signs?

If you assign each of the four elements—fire, earth, air, water—to all of the three qualities—cardinal, fixed, mutable—you come up with twelve combinations. Conversely, if you assign each of the three qualities to all of the four elements, you get the same number of combinations: twelve—the twelve signs of the zodiac. (Interesting number, 12. It keeps on turning up throughout myth, religion, and tradition. The twelve tribes of Israel, the twelve days of Christmas, the twelve apostles.)

The Greeks, with their passion for order, were the ones who pulled together the centuries of astrological tradition and created the neat and tidy system we now use for arranging the twelve signs of the zodiac according to the four elements and three qualities. Here's how they combine:

	Cardinal	Fixed	Mutable
Fire	Aries	Leo	Sagittarius
Earth	Capricorn	Taurus	Virgo
Air	Libra	Aquarius	Gemini
Water	Cancer	Scorpio	Pisces

Fire, Earth, Air, and Water

The concept of elements probably sprang naturally from early man's experience of the world and his attempts to categorize all that he saw in it, both material and nonmaterial. Comparing the ancients' notion that the four elements made up all things with our modern knowledge that there are actually more than a hundred chemical elements is as pointless as comparing eggs with apples. The early thinkers made no distinction between the solid "real" world and one's experience of that world. The elements fire, earth, air, and water might have more properly been called attributes—of a thing or a person. For instance, if something was experienced as hot rather than cold, sharp rather than dull, active rather than passive, it was said to partake primarily of the fire element. Apply those attributes to certain human personalities, and see how aptly they fit.

In Renaissance times the elements became the "humors," and were applied exclusively to personality. Fire corresponded to the humor "choler"; we still use it today in our word "choleric" (angry). Earth was the humor bile, and an excess led to a melancholy disposition. Air was the humor blood, and too much led to an overly sanguine (or rosy) outlook on life. Water was phlegm, and carried with it a personality as soggy and phlegmatic as it sounds. Shakespeare's dramas are peopled with portraits of the humors: Hamlet, the melancholy Dane, is a prime example.

Just as the elements or humors are key to the delineation of character, they play a vital role in interpersonal relationships. Though the matter of compatibility is more complex, the manner in which the elements of two people's sun signs combine with each other gives a startlingly accurate clue to how those people will get along. The most productive way to think of the astrological elements is as different kinds of energies, or as different ways of perceiving and responding to the world. There is an uncanny correspondence between the elemental or "humor" types and current descriptions of personality types as determined by psychological testing.

20

Fire corresponds to the "intuitive" personality type. Fire-sign people (Aries, Leo, Sagittarius) do not necessarily have clairvoyant ability, and none is implied by the word "intuitive." Rather, fire people are future-oriented, and prefer to see things not as they are, but as they could be. A visionary quality, enthusiasm, and optimism are three of the most delightful attributes that can often be assigned to people born under Aries, Leo, and Sagittarius.

The easiest way to remember what the element fire represents in terms of personality is to actually visualize it. Fire warms, radiates heat, aspires upward. Fire is spirit, animation, the life principle, which gives a strong sense of personal identity. Too much fire in a personality can translate into self-centeredness.

Just as fire appears to be constantly in motion, fire people are usually on the move, both literally and figuratively. There is a dynamism in fire people which initiates activity—in themselves and in other people. But there is an inherent instability in fire as well. Fire is difficult to contain, and correspondingly, fire people demand more freedom than most, and tend to chafe under restriction. The reactions of fire people are rarely tepid; they tend toward the "hotter" emotions, with all that implies.

It is not difficult to visualize the interaction of fire-sign people with those born into a different element. The air signs "fan" the fire signs and thereby intensify fire's inherent characteristics. Earth people can suffocate fire, or at least make it burn less brightly. As for the water signs, the interaction is fairly obvious: Water puts fire out.

Earth people operate on their sense perceptions: If they can see it, touch it, hear it, it is real. These are the pragmatists of the zodiac, and their reaction to things is often quite literal. The earth element adds practicality to any horoscope. For those born under an earth sign (Taurus, Virgo, Capricorn), a practical turn of mind can be a saving grace—or a cross to bear. Just as you would expect, earth gives a solid foundation to anything, and earth-sign people are often "builders"—of houses, projects, families, whatever. The earth element, according to its nature, often adds a "nurturing" quality to the personality which can be endearing. However, earth can often take away from the imagination. If one sees the world only as it is, it is difficult to carry out visions and dreams . . . or to understand the dreams of others.

If you can visualize a mound of earth pressing down upon a person, you will have an idea of why the earth element is often associated with depression, or at least a lack of joy and spontaneity in the personality. For earth people, life is lived at a pretty basic level, and creature comforts are usually mightily appreciated. This is the reason the earth signs are often dismissed as "materialistic." Not so; what they want is form and substance in their lives. Security—especially emotional—is paramount, and any threat to it makes earth-sign people anxious. On the other hand, just as earth is solid, it is patient, and can wait for things to mature—as fire cannot. The most compatible element for earth is water, because there is a natural synergy between them. Earth/water combinations may not make the world's most sparkling couples, but they can be some of the most lasting relationships.

Air is the "lightest" of the four elements, humors, or psychological types. Fire may be ebullient and outgoing, but air is more peripatetic and social. Air-sign people (Libra, Aquarius, Gemini) act out of the "thinking" principle. From this premise one might make the assumption that people born into the air signs are more intelligent than others. This is not necessarily so. What the "thinking" mode of personality entails is making connections between things and people, linking past to present and future, perceiving the world in a "linear" or logical way. In terms of brain function, it is highly probable that the air signs tend to exhibit more left-brain (rational) than right-brain (intuitive) activity.

As personalities, air-sign people seem able to be objective with less effort than other people, and more of the time. At the extreme, this can amount to total dispassion, and a seeming lack of warmth. The sociability of air-sign people derives from the nature of air itself: Air circulates, air is everywhere, air carries people, things, and ideas with it. As air is the "associating" and "connecting" element, it is the "communicating" element as well. An astonishing number of air-sign people end up in the communication trades: journalism, television, radio, writing of all kinds.

Because air has the ability to be objective, air-sign people can suffer from emotional blocks. Becoming entangled in and constricted by intense emotions is usually anathema to the air signs. The end result of this aversion is a sometimes unfortunate detachment, and difficulty in forming lasting relationships. To make air concentrate on one thing for very long is more difficult than holding nectar in a sieve. The most comfortable companion for an air-sign person is an earth-sign person, because both have a logical or practical turn of mind. The combination of air sign with fire sign is more exciting, but also more unstable.

Water is the "deepest" element, in every sense of the word. Water-sign people (Cancer, Scorpio, Pisces) look at and interpret the world in terms of their emotions; they are the natural "feelers" of the zodiac. The feeling nature of the water signs can generate tremendous creativity in all the art forms, and in life itself. Conversely, it can cause great pain—to the water-sign person himself and to others. Water penetrates; it seeps into and permeates everything. Water has considerable power when harnessed; unharnessed it can spell disaster. Water is the opposite of air, emotional where air is logical, more right-brain (intuitive) than left-brain (rational). One of the "mysterious" properties water can lend to a water-sign personality is the ability to sense what less "sensitive" souls cannot. Water-sign people can often seem to possess powers of precognition; many actually do. However, water's premonitions are often nothing more than vague forebodings about problems that never materialize. Water-sign people generally tend to take life rather seriously; perhaps they are aware, even unconsciously, of the megaton effect of their emotions—both on themselves and on others. Such power is not to be taken lightly.

It's one step from the seriousness of water to the observation that water people can be "heavy." Sometimes they are heavy in the literal sense, but more often in the sense of being less than lighthearted companions. As in all cases, the degree of "heaviness" depends on the total horoscope, rather than just the sun sign; but in general this is the case. Just as water signs tend to gravitate naturally toward the "comfortable" earth signs, they are often mistrustful of the air signs, and downright fearful of the volatile fire signs. Water may put fire out, but fire can potentially make water disappear into thin air. Aside from creativity, the most positive attribute often found in the water signs is the nurturing quality. People often turn toward the water signs in times of distress—to be lulled and rocked as in the fluid of the womb, or "cleansed" by the mystical "purifying" effect of water.

The Qualities

The astrological qualities—cardinal, fixed, and mutable—are the missing parts of the puzzle that, when filled in, reveal the twelve zodiacal signs in all their individuality. Each represents a kind of energy, movement, or direction. How precisely does a quality affect an element and combine to become a sign? It is clear when you add quality to element and see how the specific sign emerges.

Cardinal derives from the Latin word for the hinge that permits a door to open. It is appropriately descriptive of the *initiatory* nature of the four cardinal signs: Aries, Cancer, Libra, and Capricorn. Cardinal signs *start* things—each according to its element—and it is no coincidence that they are the signs that "open" each of the four seasons of the year. The cardinal movement is forward, and the direction is straight ahead.

However their energy manifests itself, cardinal signs are movers and shakers, and you will very often find them in the position of "moving force" behind enterprises.

Cardinal quality + *Fire* element = *Aries*
Aries is the most cardinal of the cardinals, coming appropriately at the very opening of the entire zodiac. Like all fire signs, Aries is active and dynamic; as a cardinal sign, Aries often puts that energy into starting things—sometimes finishing little. Even so, people rally round this sign. You are aware in the presence of Aries that there's a natural leader among you; just where he will take you is another matter.

Cardinal quality + *Water* element = *Cancer*

The reason Cancer is often able to overcome the water signs' tendency to shy away from the new is that it partakes of the cardinal quality. Cancer may be fearful, yet Cancer moves forward. It should be no surprise that Cancer, so often described as a domestic stay-at-home, is a sign that turns up frequently on the "most successful" list in business and professions.

Cardinal quality + *Air* element = *Libra*

Libra can be another surprising sign—again, because of its cardinality. If your natural penchant is to initiate things, you can't stay on the fence forever. The problem is that affable Libra's strong forward direction is often masked. Desiring to please all and offend no one, Libra can steal the prize and run away with it while you aren't looking.

Cardinal quality + *Earth* element = *Capricorn*

The sign that opens the winter season is often labeled "materialistic." As a cardinal sign, Capricorn moves forward; as an earth sign, Capricorn moves steadily toward the more solid and tangible things of this world. Capricorn's cardinal direction is possibly the most powerful, though Capricorn is less flamboyant than Aries and less calculated than Libra.

Fixed is the quality of the signs that fall in the middle of each season. It goes something like this: The cardinal signs start the action, and the fixed signs consolidate the position. As the word implies, the fixed signs are more stable in their way than either the cardinal or the mutable signs. Because the motion or direction of fixed signs is basically static, centrifugal, or "in place," it is also much more difficult to move, change, or unseat them. The fixed signs are sometimes called the "executive" signs, with good reason.

Fixed quality + *Fire* element = *Leo*
The reason Leo is often extolled as the ideal manager or parent is that this active, warm fire sign burns with a "fixed" or steady heat. Leo stands in the center, and all else pivots around him; you always know where Leo stands. The notable loyalty of Leo also derives from the fixed quality: Once Leo's light shines on you, it will shine forever.

Fixed quality + *Earth* element = *Taurus*
Why is Taurus often described as stubborn? Simple: It's even harder to move the solid earth of Taurus because it is "fixed" in one place. However, when you combine the palpable element earth with the unmoving quality of fixity, you come up with a pretty sturdy character, and one to be counted upon.

Fixed quality + *Water* element = *Scorpio*
The tremendous reserve of many Scorpios can be attributed to the fact that Scorpio is a "fixed" sign. Water's depth of feeling and emotion is tightly contained in one place, and virtually immovable. What this also means is that Scorpios tend toward grudge-keeping and possessiveness; they hold on to ideas and people to the death.

Fixed quality + *Air* element = *Aquarius*
The Aquarian tends to be much less a will o' the wisp than the other air signs, Gemini and Libra. People born under the fixed air sign can better concentrate their abilities—both social and communicative. Their ideas are often both lofty and

sound at one time; fixity gives a firm base for logic. Aquarians often display these tendencies as social reformers and political activists.

Mutable is virtually a synonym for "flexible." The signs that fall at the end of each season are beginning to feel the necessity to move out of the way for the next cardinal sign. The mutable signs' motion is a kind of spiral, or a zigzag pattern resembling broken-field running. Naturally this makes the mutable signs more adaptable than the other signs of the same element, a most valuable asset in social relationships. Unfortunately, mutability also makes these signs a bit less stable and reliable.

Mutable quality + *Fire* element = *Sagittarius*
Sometimes rash and as easily riled as the other fire signs, Sagittarius is more able to forgive and forget than Aries or Leo. Mutable signs "bend." Sagittarians can sometimes bend others out of shape by erratic behavior and "spaced-out" episodes. The reason: their fiery visions come so thick and fast it is difficult for some Sagittarians to communicate them clearly or stick with them for long.

Mutable quality + *Earth* element = *Virgo*
All the earth signs tend toward anxiety, but mutable Virgo can be the most anxious of all. Virgos constantly shift attention from practical concern to practical concern, often causing themselves endless worry. There is a constant need to make this world and everything in it better, more workable, closer to perfect.

Mutable quality + *Air* element = *Gemini*
Since air is constantly circulating anyway, Gemini's mutable or "flexible" quality makes this air sign

appear flighty at times. On the other hand, an easygoing manner and genial adaptability make Gemini one of the most delightful companions in the zodiac. A super ability to connect with lots of ideas often makes Gemini a prolific writer, particularly of comedy.

Mutable quality + *Water* element = *Pisces*
The flowing, merging, fluid character of water as both symbol and reality is emphasized in Pisces to the point of taking over the personality. The Piscean's often deserved reputation for unreliability is an unfortunate manifestation of this element/quality combination. On the plus side, however, Pisces' malleability is a fantastic boon to the actor, who must project constantly changing emotions, and to the therapist, who must grasp and interpret them.

3. WHAT SEX IS YOUR SIGN?

A little more than a decade ago, the women's liberation movement erupted on our social scene and changed the way we regard "women's place." More recently, "house husbands" and other nontraditional occupations have appeared, liberating males from stereotypes. This sex-role revolution is one factor leading many to believe we have already entered the "Age of Aquarius," when accepted modes of living will seem to turn upside down. Are we witnessing chaos, or is this gradual closing of the gender gap a return to the way things were meant to be? Once again, astrology has something revealing and cogent to say.

The "Third Sex"

There is an ancient astrological myth that contends there were originally three sexes—male, female, and androgyne. This last was a perfect balance of male and female. Created by the gods as children of the sun, moon, and earth, the three sexes had varying degrees of power by virtue of their parental heritage. The androgynes, possessing both sun (male) and moon (female) characteristics, were the most powerful, and therefore the most threatening to Zeus. Instead of destroying the androgynes, he decided to "split" them into male and female segments. Since then, the myth tells us, the two sexes as we know them have wandered the earth looking for their other and sometimes better half. From this ancient wisdom, revealed as many truths are through myth, we can draw the conclusion that "androgyny" is the desired human condition, and that all of us suffer by our one-sex-to-a-person state.

It is important to establish that we are not talking of sex in the physical, bodily sense, but of *gender*—that is, the qualities of maleness and femaleness as they manifest themselves in outlook and attitudes. The bisexual is not the same as the androgyne, whose nature contains both male and female attributes in perfect balance. Some claim that Jesus Christ was the prototypical androgyne, capable of both great force and great mercy.

The Sex of the Signs

The zodiac is divided into male and female signs. It starts with a masculine sign, Aries, and continues with Taurus, a feminine sign. The subsequent signs alternate male and female throughout the rest of the zodiac.

Masculine signs		Feminine signs	
Aries	Libra	Taurus	Scorpio
Leo	Aquarius	Virgo	Pisces
Sagittarius	Gemini	Capricorn	Cancer

In astrological and other "occult" tradition, the first and primal division of all things is into the polarities, or opposites: masculine and feminine. Everything in the universe partakes of either the male/Yang/active/"plus" principle or the female/Yin/passive/"minus" principle. The polarities are *complementary*, each necessary to the existence of the other. Far from representing a "better" or "worse," each combines with the other to form a perfect whole. The words "positive" and "negative" are another way of expressing the fundamental meaning of polarity, and the photograph is a useful image. The photograph itself is the positive; it is taken from and made possible by the negative. The two are different parts of the same reality. The difference is that the positive is the "light," more visible, more affirming part, and the negative the "dark" and more or less silent part.

The original symbol of the masculine polarity was the sun, so part of maleness is living in the direct light of day, the "outer world," so to speak, and utilizing the direct, left-brain mode of perception. The archetypal symbol of the feminine polarity is the moon, so, correspondingly, femaleness means living in the reflected light of the sun, dwelling in the "inner world," drawing upon "dark," unconscious, right-brain insights.

If these definitions are beginning to sound like our contemporary stereotypes of "the man" and "the woman," it is no accident. But why are some signs masculine and some signs feminine? A look at the elements gives some clues. The fire and air signs are masculine by virtue of their outer-directed, outgoing, initiating, dynamic nature; they dwell on the "light" side of the cosmic equation. The earth and water signs are feminine because in general they are less flamboyant, more inner-directed, "softer," more indrawn. Their nature corresponds to the "dark" or negative side of that same equation. As in photography, it is the positive we see most clearly as opposed to the negative.

To sum up the root meanings of "maleness" and "femaleness":

Masculine	*Feminine*
Yang	Yin
Active	Passive
Plus	Minus
Positive	Negative
Outer	Inner
Conscious	Unconscious
Left-brain-oriented	Right-brain-oriented
Solar	Lunar
Assertive	Retiring
Self-expressive	Self-repressive
Direct	Indirect
Straightforward	Subtle

And on and on, into any other "polarities" you can name, from hot/cold to rough/smooth to hard/soft.

It should by now be obvious why the androgynes were considered both close to perfect and more powerful than their one-sex sisters and brothers. Earth's original "third sex" had the whole range of maleness and femaleness at its fingertips, and could draw easily upon *both* sides of the cosmos—be both the positive and the negative of the photograph at will. In our limited one-sex-to-a-person world it is harder to achieve that balance and hence that power, but it is nevertheless available to anyone, male or female, regardless of physical sex or zodiacal sun sign.

Right-Sex vs. Wrong-Sex

Since the characteristics of your sun sign are the ones most accessible to you in directing your life and your destiny, the designation of signs as "male" or "female" seems to point to a dilemma: What happens when you are born into a sign opposite to your physical sex?

The bad news is that almost inevitably there is a measure of psychic discomfort. The male-sign woman and the female-sign man often feel they do not "fit in their own skin." For instance, fire-sign and air-sign females, while usually successful in the business and professional worlds, often have difficulty playing the traditional female role in relationships. Correspondingly, water-sign and earth-sign males may assert themselves badly, and secretly desire to refrain from the competition that daily life makes necessary.

The good news for wrong-sex-sign people is that they are much more able to close the "gender gap" within them and evolve toward wholeness, or androgyny. Masculine-sign men may find it easier to be "typically male," and feminine-sign women to be "typically female," but all too often they are one-sided—overly attuned to the masculine or feminine vibrations of the universe. In our role-changing world, it is far from a compliment to be described as "all man" or "all woman."

The road to male/female completeness is made rockier by social conditioning. Boys are obviously endowed physically with the outer "male" part of the connection and girls with the perfect female "socket," and this tends to categorize their roles from the start. In spite of the great strides made by both men and women in recent years, sex-typing is still an unfortunate fact of contemporary life—unfortunate because it imposes a false limitation on our total capabilities as human beings. Astrology offers some interesting ways to develop your "missing half" and come closer to total personhood. One route is via the sibling system.

The Sibling System

The twelve signs of the zodiac, from Aries through Pisces, not only alternate sex, they also represent a "growing-up" process from childhood through old age. That means each astrological sign has an older "brother" or "sister." For instance, Aries, the youngest sign, represents the primal urge to be, the headlong rush into life. Big sister Taurus provides the balance, with less activity, more stability, the urge to nurture rather than to sow. Feminine Pisces, the last and "oldest" sign, is theoretically the wisest, having accumulated the whole of human experience. World-weary Pisces, therefore, looks ahead to young Aries for rejuvenation, and the round starts again.

Since one can meet as many immature Pisces people as "grown-up" Aries people, it is wise not to take the ages of the signs too literally. However, in attempting to overcome "gender gap," it can be extremely helpful for anyone to look to his or her older sibling. Whether you are born into a sign of the "right sex" or the "wrong sex," there are valuable lessons to be learned by observing the sign that comes directly after your own.

Aries:
Masculine Fire

Polarity, Taurus:
Feminine Earth

The Male: Your constant itch to get things moving can make you feisty and unnecessarily abrupt. Look to Taurus to cultivate patience and develop the ability to bide your time. Your "fast-start" syndrome would bear much better results if you learned to build things one brick at a time, the way Taurus does. Also, your interpersonal relationships might go more smoothly if you learned how to give some Taurean TLC.

The Female: Your Taurus sister instinctively knows when to take a back seat, hence often fares better in affairs of the heart than you do. You can make men feel they've got to win to win you; observe how subtly Taurus deals with her competitive urge. Don't be concerned about practicing passivity. Your sign has endowed you with enough get-up-and-go for two people. Don't lose your "buddy-buddy" tomboy charm in the process, however.

Taurus:	*Polarity, Gemini:*
Feminine Earth	*Masculine Air*

The Male: You may sometimes feel at a disadvantage in the presence of more flamboyant peers. The easiest way for you to even up the situation is to get a bit more verbal. You've got plenty of good ideas that rest on a firm foundation; learning to put them across with some wit and sparkle like Gemini could put you in the driver's seat. Never underestimate your powers of attraction: Your soft-edge sun sign makes you especially attractive to women, not to mention dogs and children.

The Female: You may be too much of the ideal woman for your own good. For one thing, men may take advantage of your patience and make you wait, certain you'll always be there. Take a lesson from more assertive Gemini, and turn the tables—even at the risk of a relationship. Your intense sexuality guarantees you'll never lack a partner. However, your Gemini sister does a few things better than you do; watch the way she circulates and self-promotes, both on the job and on the town.

Gemini:
Masculine Air

Polarity, Cancer:
Feminine Water

The Male: With your skim-the-surface air, you can come across as "brittle." Take a leaf from Cancer's book and try occasionally to be the "strong, silent type." As popular as you may be, you may not be eligible for the best-partner award, on either the home or the office front. Get in touch with some of Cancer's warmth and sensitivity; the Cancer male knows how to do it without getting overly sentimental.

The Female: Gemini women are usually highly visible—and audible. However, they are not always soft to the touch, in a manner of speaking. Your Cancerian sister has her own problems, but this is not usually one of them. Watch how she uses her Cancerian sensitivity to make people feel comfortable with her. As a female in a male sign, you've got an edge, however. You can compete with the best of them—but your "soft side" should never be too far away.

Cancer:
Feminine Water

Polarity, Leo:
Masculine Fire

The Male: There is a saying that Cancer fathers make the best mothers. The why of it is simple: As a male, the Cancerian is programmed to be authoritative; as a Cancer, he is instinctively attuned to the attributes of the feminine polarity, including the urge to nurture and protect. This is a pretty powerful combination in any area of life, but the self-doubting Cancer male could use a large dose of Leo's instinctive self-assurance.

The Female: In the Cancer female it is possible to find a living example of the often-parodied Jewish mother, regardless of ethnic origin. Where the male Cancer can direct with authority, the female Cancer may manipulate with emotionalism—even unwittingly. Her more self-assured Leo sister rallies people round her by being somebody they can lean on. The Cancer woman should never forget her sign is a cardinal one—which means that, like Leo, she has it in her to lead instead of merely follow.

Leo:	*Polarity, Virgo:*
Masculine Fire	*Feminine Earth*

The Male: In the Leo male the fires of idealism and ambition may burn so brightly that he neglects the less glamorous realities of a situation. The feminine sign Virgo—his astrological older sister—has the "womanly" attribute of sitting back and reflecting, picking up the possible flaws that can lead to a downfall for Leo. For some women, Leo males are not hard to resist: They come on so strong it's a turn-off. The retiring quality of feminine Virgo is a good model to follow for counterbalance.

The Female: Strong, loyal Leo, with all its leadership qualities, is a natural to find among women executives. Leo women can be "the boss" with little effort. On the other hand, they can lack insight into the more subtle factors of dealing with employees, peers, and even their own bosses. Leo's Virgo sister is far more canny, always keeping her eye on the ball. Leo women may succeed in business without trying, but in love it's a different matter. Giving out with a fiery rush of emotion right at the start can lead to disillusionment. Older sister Virgo is disillusioned from the start.

Virgo:
Feminine Earth

Polarity, Libra:
Masculine Air

The Male: Here's a case where "gender gap" can have fairly serious consequences. The Virgo male is often the perfect underling, the perpetual follower, the legendary "bridesmaid" who never becomes a bride. The feminine urge to self-repress meshes too perfectly with the Virgo nature, and it is quite difficult for the male Virgo to tap his self-assertive natural resources. Big brother Libra is an ideal role model, since he can move ahead of others and achieve without ruffling feathers or becoming abrasive.

The Female: Obviously the above applies in spades to the Virgo female. She can suffer from the painful anxiety that comes of trying to be the perfect servant in an imperfect world. Whatever her occupation or role, unfounded fears of failing can amount to paranoia. The lesson to be learned from Libra is objectivity: Virgo women should learn to say, "what is really going on here . . . what is really expected of me?" The other Libra secret for Virgo: Relax and take time to smell the roses.

Libra:
Masculine Air

Polarity, Scorpio:
Feminine Water

The Male: As a sign, Libra is a bit of an anomaly—masculine, yet oddly "soft-edge." The paradox stems from Libra's rulership by the lovely planet Venus. As a result, Libra males have a great blend of natural and astrological equipment. Where they can come a cropper is in appearing to lack conviction, about both ideas and people. Libra's lack of intensity has its polar opposite in Scorpio, the sign the male Libra should look to for guidance. Along with intensity, Scorpio possesses a natural tenacity, something lackadaisical Libra could use a dose of.

The Female: The planet Venus also comes to the aid of the female Libra, giving her a romantic aura that is often irresistible. Yet airlike Libra can resist very well, often too well. The female Libran can suffer from lack of involvement—a sometimes disturbing tendency to remain cool when others heat up. Both in romance and in business, Libra females might fare better if they emulated "older" Scorpios, who fling themselves into the fray, becoming totally involved, living life both more intensely and more interestingly.

Scorpio:	*Polarity, Sagittarius:*
Feminine Water	*Masculine Fire*

The Male: The emotionalism of the water signs has more serious consequences in Scorpio, who all too often can "play the heavy," usually by holding on to everything—including the "darker" emotions like jealousy and suspicion. The male Scorpio's ideal role model is Sagittarius, who is far more able to let go and adopt a philosophical attitude toward life's inevitable disappointments. "Heavy" can also describe Scorpio's mood a great deal of the time; a healthy dose of Sagittarian optimism could do wonders.

The Female: Generally more liked by men than by women, the Scorpio female can overplay her own sex role. Scorpio women sometimes fancy themselves *femmes fatales* because of the emotional episodes that may occur with regularity in their relationship lives. Truth is, men as well as women eventually turn off, looking for a lighter partner. Scorpio's older-brother sign, Sagittarius,

offers an answer: Start shooting for the stars instead of
staring at your navel.

Sagittarius: **Polarity, Capricorn:**
Masculine Fire **Feminine Earth**

The Male: This likable and lively sign produces some
of the friendliest types in the zodiac. The Sagittarian
male may run into problems as a manager, however,
when he finds it necessary to lay down the law. His
uppermost concern is likely to be congeniality rather
than productivity. The next sign, Capricorn, is much
tougher—and, therefore, a good person for Sagittarius
to watch. Although a touch less interesting, Capricorn
has more staying power in relationships than Sagittarius
as well.

The Female: The Sagittarian woman can be confusing
to the opposite sex: Does she want to be a buddy or a
sweetheart? Usually the Sagittarian female herself does
not know; the only thing she's sure of is that she doesn't
want to be fenced in, because life is so full of marvelous
possibilities. Older-sister sign Capricorn can chime in
sensibly with the most male of male conversations, but
she never forgets the skin she's in. A dash of Capricorn
stability could be a great boon to the slapdash Sagittarian's modus operandi, as well.

Capricorn: **Polarity, Aquarius:** ·
Feminine Earth **Masculine Air**

The Male: One of the zodiac's more solid citizens, the
Capricorn male can usually be counted on, no matter
what the duty or obligation. People sometimes wish he
were a bit less predictable and a lot more exciting,
however. While Capricorn is a consummate doer and

41

achiever, the feminine nature of the sign makes the Capricorn male rather self-repressive. Aquarius, his sibling sign, can strike a balance. Mature Aquarians are rarely truly unconventional, but they know how and when to stray from the beaten track and make life more interesting.

The Female: A natural "success sign," Capricorn breeds some of our most achieving female executives; it also produces some pretty lonely ladies. Capricorn women, like the men, take life very seriously, and seem to believe even one's love life takes a lot of hard work. That life is real, sibling-sign Aquarius will never deny; what Aquarius knows better than Capricorn, however, is that there's a big wonderful world out there. Capricorn women should take the time to cultivate some interesting interests outside the home or office.

| *Aquarius:* | *Polarity, Pisces:* |
| *Masculine Air* | *Feminine Water* |

The Male: Theoretically, Aquarius should be a very communicative sign, belonging as it does to the air element. However, one problem with Aquarians in general and male Aquarians in particular is that they will communicate about everything in the world except their own feelings. Sometimes one wonders if they really have them. They do, of course, but dealing with emotion is something bordering on frightening for the male Aquarian. "Sob sister" Pisces may go overboard in the other direction, but provides a useful model for the Aquarian man who has trouble finding his feelings.

The Female: As youngsters, Aquarian girls usually have no lack of playmates. Later on, however, they may begin to feel left out—especially by men. No matter how charming, lively, sparkling, and/or witty she is, the female Aquarian may have few intimates. The hurly-burly of close emotional ties, with men or women, she leaves to others—like her Pisces sister. By studying a Pisces the Aquarian female can observe the receptive feminine nature at its deepest, and learn to project warmth and sympathy herself.

Pisces:	*Polarity, Aries:*
Feminine Water	*Masculine Fire*

The Male: It is sad but true that many Piscean males drift through life with little apparent direction. This in part derives from the fact that it is the most feminine of the feminine signs, in the sense of lacking self-assertion. Though you may be able to point to exceptions, it is generally true that male Pisceans are "receivers" rather than "transmitters." In boisterous, energetic Aries lies Pisces' salvation. The first sign of the zodiac is virtually antithetical to the last, and though Aries may jar Pisces' nerves, Pisces would do well to take a leaf from Aries' book.

The Female: In general, Pisces females fare better than the men of this sign. That is, however, if they stick to pretty traditional female roles. In fact, if the Piscean woman gives in to her ultranegative polarity, she can be the classic clinging vine. There is generally a great deal of creativity, but it needs focusing. Some Piscean females focus too much on creating babies. Their older-sibling sign Aries provides the perfect role model by being direct, outgoing, and "courageous" in the sense of meeting life head on.

43

4. WHICH HOUSE IS YOUR HOME?

A horoscope or natal map looks like a pie divided into twelve sections, or a wheel with twelve spokes. The sections are called "houses" and the spokes that divide them are called "cusps." Since the wheel makes a complete turn every twenty-four hours (actually, the daily rotation of the earth), the positions of the planets between the spokes change. The total meaning of your horoscope is therefore tremendously affected by which planets are in which houses at the moment of your birth. The astrologer views your natal map, or picture of the sky, as a freeze frame in a film. It represents one particular moment in the continuing drama of time: your moment.

That is why it is important to know your time of birth as closely as possible. Family records, your birth certificate, and the Bureau of Vital Statistics in your state are all sources you can try. For the purposes of this chapter, if you know the two-hour period within the twenty-four-hour day in which you were born, you can determine which house the sun was in at the moment of your birth, and hence which house is your "home."

Each house of the horoscope represents a different facet of the total human experience. Put another way, each house of the horoscope is a "slice of life," and the twelve slices add up to all there is for us here on earth. If you keep in mind that your sun sign is the real "you"

44

and the sun is your "essence," you can appreciate the fact that the house that contains your sun has the greatest importance in the direction of your life.

The house of your sun sign is your "home" because it indicates the particular area of human experience in which you will play out your role this lifetime.

In the interlocking pattern of symbols that is astrology, each horoscope house corresponds to a zodiac sign and a planet. If you remember the metaphor used in an earlier chapter, the planet (in this case the sun) is the actor, the sign is the costume and makeup he wears, and the house is the particular stage set in which the action takes place. Each house also has a polarity or sex, just as the signs do. The planets, signs, and houses line up as follows:

Planet	Sign	House	Polarity
Mars	Aries	First	Positive/masculine
Venus	Taurus	Second	Negative/feminine
Mercury	Gemini	Third	Positive/masculine
Moon	Cancer	Fourth	Negative/feminine
Sun	Leo	Fifth	Positive/masculine
Mercury	Virgo	Sixth	Negative/feminine
Venus	Libra	Seventh	Positive/masculine
Pluto	Scorpio	Eighth	Negative/feminine
Jupiter	Sagittarius	Ninth	Positive/masculine
Saturn	Capricorn	Tenth	Negative/feminine
Uranus	Aquarius	Eleventh	Positive/masculine
Neptune	Pisces	Twelfth	Negative/feminine

Another general way of classifying the houses is as follows:

- Houses one, five, and nine: "personal" houses
- Houses two, six, and ten: "practical" houses
- Houses three, seven, and eleven: "social" houses

- Houses four, eight, and twelve: "unconscious" or "subconscious" houses

You might notice that these house classifications also roughly correspond to the elements, fire, earth, air, and water; that too is no accident.

The fact that your sun probably falls into a different house than the one that corresponds to your sun sign does not mean that you "become" that sign. Rather your house "colors" your life, and the way you live out your sun sign. For instance, if your sun sign is Taurus and your sun falls into the ninth house, the house of Sagittarius, it can mean that you will be the kind of Taurean personality who tends to live life on a broader and deeper level than the "pure" Taurean might.

Important! In looking for the house that corresponds to the two-hour period during which you were born, remember to take daylight saving time into account. If you have any doubts about whether or not daylight saving was in effect when you were born, a quick call to a community or state office will settle the matter.

Born between 4 and 6 a.m.—SUN IN THE FIRST HOUSE

Predawn-to-dawn births are fairly common, so many people may find that the first house is their home. Not a bad place for the sun to reside, all things considered. It is the house of *self*, and no matter what your sun sign may be, this placement lends you the opportunity to express your individuality in a positive way. In fact, "negative" or self-repressive signs may end up in the spotlight in spite of themselves with the sun placed here. Because the natural ruler of the first house is Mars, there is a kind of jet propulsion experienced here—and for some it may be uncomfortable. For others, it may be all too compatible with their natural bent.

The fire signs particularly should beware of a tendency to arrogance when the sun falls into the first house. The fiery sun further ignited by fiery Mars can create overkill in terms of the individual's sense of self. More literally, a fire sun in a fire house is a dangerous combination; most accidents are caused by impatience and impetuosity.

In general, people with the sun in the first house have a fairly clear self-image, at least once youth is past. That image may be "good" or it may be "bad"; the point is that first-house-sun people are *aware* of themselves and the personalities they project. Since respect and recognition are first-house goals, the first-house-sun person will at least try to present himself or herself in a way that is acceptable to others—or that attains his or her ends. Regardless of your sun sign, if the first house is your "home" you will experience a "cosmic itch" to be out front. A first-house sun doesn't guarantee that you will get anywhere, but it does mean you won't fail for lack of interest.

Born between 2 and 4 a.m.—SUN IN THE SECOND HOUSE

If the first-house-sun individual wants recognition, the second-house-sun person wants something far more tangible. This is the house of material possessions and security, in all senses of the word. Even a "flaky" horoscope is strengthened by a second-house sun, which places the individual in the earning/gaining/owning area of human experience. The life work may literally be banking, finance, or commodities; at any rate the life goals are likely to be sustenance and substance. Part of the effect of having the sun in the second house is to want things very badly—and to have the persistence to pursue them and get what you want. In the case of the second-house-sun person it is virtually assured, if the sun sign is reasonably strong.

As one can imagine, the earth signs and to some extent the water signs feel most "at home" in this house. The solid parameters of the second house mesh quite well with their instincts to build, preserve, and hold on. For some—particularly Taurus and Capricorn—a second-house sun may lead to an excessive desire for and concern with the material. For the fire signs, who tend to rush forward with little regard for the material consequences, a second-house sun can be a godsend, and the ticket to fortune if not fame. Fire possesses the ideas, the foresight, and the enthusiasm to succeed; the second house acts both as a much-needed "brake" and as a practical foundation. If the second house sounds a bit dull, it is. People with sun in the second house, regardless of sun sign, would do well to make an effort to broaden their horizons and look beyond merely the here and now.

Born between midnight and 2 a.m.—SUN IN THE THIRD HOUSE

Coming as it does in the first quarter of the wheel of the horoscope, the third house represents our early environment and the first relationships we form. It is sometimes called the house of brothers and sisters. What that means for the third-house-sun person is a desire to communicate, teach, and learn in a fairly basic way—the way we learned from and taught our siblings. In the world of work, many third-house-sun people may play out their career roles as schoolteachers, and writers of news, light prose, and humor.

The third house is also called the house of short journeys. In the life of the individual this often works out as a concern with what is nearby and immediate rather than what is way out there. Third-house-sun people put a high priority on their environment in terms of the kinds of people they want around them. It is a highly congenial house, coming as it does under the rulership of Mercury and Gemini. Sociability will be "forced" on the third-house-sun person who would really rather be reclusive. Even a relatively noncommunicative sign like Scorpio will "lighten up" and breathe fresher air in the third house. The third is also called one of the "mental" houses, and this should be a cautionary note for the air signs, Gemini, Libra and Aquarius. "Cool" and logical by nature, they can be positively chilly in this house; feelings should be cultivated. For all signs, going, coming, talking, writing, communicating, and socializing are the worldly things this house represents. It is in every way a "positive" house for the sun, because it puts us in direct contact with our fellow creatures, and in general smooths our contacts with them.

Born between 10 p.m. and midnight—SUN IN THE FOURTH HOUSE

The first, fourth, and tenth houses of the horoscope are particularly strong placements for the sun, and you find the sun there in many achieving horoscopes. For the fourth-house-sun person, worldly achievement may not always come easily, however, for this house is at the very bottom of the horoscope, and it takes effort to break out of it into the upper or outer reaches of life. The fourth house represents our parental home, the "nest" where our most ingrained and subconscious habits were formed. The fourth house is a comfortable place, and one can desire to stay there forever. It is a bit like the womb, and for some people, leaving it is as traumatic as birth. This is particularly true for the water signs, and to some extent for the earth signs. Their natural inertia and in some cases fear can make them cling and want to "stay home" forever. That, however, is the neurotic reaction, and most normal people with fourth-house suns do indeed enter the world—and sometimes compensate by their choice of role or profession. For instance, the fourth-house-sun woman can be the perfect stay-at-home homemaker and mother. Some signs choose the "helping" professions, such as nursing, therapy, or counseling, and thereby act out their desire to be mothered by mothering.

Whatever the sun sign, it will color the person especially vividly when the sun falls into the fourth house. There is tremendous energy here, though of a subterranean nature. It can catapult the fire signs to positions of great power and authority, though they may never feel fully comfortable with their "exposed" condition. For fourth-house-sun people the desire to retreat will always be strong.

Born between 8 and 10 p.m.—SUN IN THE FIFTH HOUSE

The keynote for the fifth house is self-expression. It differs from the first house in that the desire to make an individual statement is even stronger here—and the likelihood of making it is even greater. The fifth house—the "natural" house of Leo—can almost literally be called a stage, and an astonishing number of performers have sun in the fifth. The stamp of individuality can be put on many things by fifth-house-sun people—books, paintings, newsworthy feats, even scandalous behavior. For many people, what they "create" that bears their stamp is children. The fifth house is a wonderful placement for parents, as long as their sun sign contains the qualities of warmth and emotion. Early-education teachers are often fifth-house-sun people, and the nursery or classroom becomes their "stage."

Like the first house, the fifth sometimes forces negative signs to take a chance on life and show their natural colors publicly. Life is a gamble for anyone, but fifth-house-sun people often find that fact positively enjoyable. Literal gambling for some can become an addiction. More amorous types with fifth-house suns work out their speculative fever by taking a chance on love—often. The fifth is often called the house of romance and love affairs (as opposed to marriage, which is the province of the seventh house). The pleasure principle is a strong component of fifth-house activity, and an aspect of it that certain self-indulgent types should take seriously. There is a light note to everything connected with the fifth house, and that is not a derogatory statement. Life should be pleasurable no matter what route we follow. If all parents could learn to "play" as fifth-house-sun people do, most children would be a lot better off. The real "danger" of the fifth house is self-glorification, and fire signs particularly should watch out for this tendency.

Born between 6 and 8 p.m.—SUN IN THE SIXTH HOUSE

By contrast with the fifth house, the sixth strikes a somewhat somber note: It is the house of duty, responsibility, and service. The natural house of Virgo, the sixth house is the natural arena of "number two" people or those in backup positions. For the earth signs particularly, the sixth house is a comfortable place to hide—and there is surely nothing wrong with a life of service and dedication to a job, a person, or an idea. The problem for the earth-sign person particularly is that without some "grace notes" in his or her horoscope,

51

all work and no play can mean a rather dull existence. There is a theory, according to the law of karma, that the sixth house is where we "pay for" the possible excesses of the fifth.

A more positive manifestation of the sixth house is efficiency. Sixth-house-sun people often have a built-in necessity to make things, people, and families work—and work well. The word "necessity" is the key, however, and many sixth-house-sun people may feel they are constantly pushing the proverbial rock uphill. This can be particularly true of the fire and air signs, who both want freedom of movement. The sixth house to some of them can seem like a "prison"; but their efforts to break out can often bear interesting and fruitful results. The fire sign in an earth house can be a dynamo of activity and production.

When disheartened, a sixth-house-sun person can feel drained, both physically and mentally. It is also known as the house of health, and a concern for the physical body can lead to hypochondria if allowed to run wild. On the positive side, sixth-house-sun people can have such a great interest in health and nutrition that it provides a life's work. Many nutritionists, physical therapists, lab researchers, and pharmacists have sixth-house suns. Some sixth-house-sun people serve so well in their chosen roles that they are singled out for commendation and/or promotion—and are less than comfortable with the attention.

Born between 4 and 6 p.m.—SUN IN THE SEVENTH HOUSE

The seventh house is exactly 180 degrees away from the first house, so, as the keynote for the first is "I," the keynote for the seventh is "we." This is the house of partnership and shared experience. In terms of totality of the horoscope, it is this house where we must "learn" that there are other people in the world. For many seventh-house-sun people this is a "given"; the concept is not difficult to deal with at all, and they are perfectly comfortable knowing they are one-half of a perfect whole. This is particularly true of the air signs, who see the logic of the situation and "know" that it is both desirable and productive to have a partner in many aspects of life. Whatever is good for one is even better for two, reasons the air sign. Even "distant" Aquarius, who may not necessarily marry, will always hook up with a group or an ideal that complements him.

Obviously, then, the "loner" signs like Aries and Scorpio are going to be unhappy in the seventh house. Since it is the house of marriage, the seventh house can be an uncomfortable home for those who want to rule the roost, regardless of sun sign. Indeed, the placement of the sun in the seventh house is often an indication of a "stronger" partner. For leaners, this is ideal; for leaders, it can spell trouble. Acceptance is the answer, for both parties to the seventh-house-sun relationship. The seventh house starts the "upper half" of the horoscope, which represents the real world, and that we are not alone in that world is an incontrovertible fact of life. Seventh-house-sun people can be superb in business and the professions, as employers, employees, and peers.

Born between 2 and 4 p.m.—SUN IN THE EIGHTH HOUSE

The house of "death and transformation" is a pretty heavy handle, but the eighth house is actually a rather good placement for the sun. The rulership of Pluto lends depth and power to this house, and though its "inhabitants" may have to share with others, they often benefit from them. Legacies and inheritances are connected with this house, and though you may never actually receive one, the practical application is that you might find your life's work in handling other people's money—a job you would do well.

"Other people's resources" is one of the taglines of this house, and "resources" means more things than money. Deep-looking eighth-house-sun people may show great acumen in psychoanalytic and/or therapeutic work. The "death and transformation" part takes earthly form in the fact that eighth-house-sun people can deal with "endings" in a positive way, sometimes turning what might be discarded into something of value. Cases in point: Undertakers and waste-disposal firms come under eighth-house rulership. More common eighth-house "endings" are the transition from childhood to parenthood and the single state to marriage.

What characterizes the eighth-house-sun person is deep commitment. Each stage or station of life is taken with great seriousness and ceremony, and there is a high degree of dedication. What this means is that an eighth-house placement can add needed depth to the "lighter" sun signs. Conversely, it can make the more freedom-loving signs feel claustrophobic. In a sense, one might call the eighth the house of "true responsibility," and as such it can be a bit oppressive.

Born between noon and 2 p.m.—SUN IN THE NINTH HOUSE

Falling under the rulership of Jupiter and Sagittarius, the ninth house is both broad and long, metaphorically speaking. It is the house of understanding, higher education, publishing, and long-distance travel. People with sun in the ninth may literally teach at college level, write, delve into philosophy and metaphysics, or work in foreign countries; or they may also simply take symbolic journeys into the far and wide. There is an expansiveness to the ninth house that is good for almost any sun sign; though for some, like Pisces, there may just be too much room to move around in and consequently they may find it harder to find a direction. For the most part, however, ninth-house-sun people feel a kind of internal freedom; they have the sense that boundaries are to be leaped over, and that they can do it—if only mentally.

Idealism and religious fervor are part of the ninth-house scene. In the great majority of people this will act as pure background to their lives in the here and now—although the desire to uplift others is often present in ninth-house-sun people. And of course, the danger of being preachy is always present as well. Fire signs are the most compatible with this house and water signs the least. Since it is the house of higher thought and the air signs are mental, they are fairly comfortable in the ninth as well. In fact, an air sign with the sun in the ninth house is the perfect combination for someone who wants to go into publishing. In sum, the ninth house is the place you will find many of the broad-minded people in this world.

Born between 10 a.m. and noon—SUN IN THE TENTH HOUSE

Along with the first and the fourth, this is one of the true "power" houses of the zodiac. It stands at the very top or zenith of the horoscope, and in astrological tradition kings and other "supermen" have sun in the tenth house. It is, in fact, uncanny how many people born near noon do achieve fame—or notoriety.

The tenth house is like the tip of the iceberg, that part the rest of the world sees. It is the house of prestige, or lack of it, because it is here in the symbolic round of the horoscope that one confronts the outer world. The tenth house stands for one's calling or vocation, and one's success or failure in it.

For some people, to be born with the sun in the tenth house is a mixed blessing. The potential of this house is so great it is hard for anyone to live up to it, and those with the sun in the tenth house will feel driven to achieve. Without a good, solid foundation in the rest of the horoscope, it is easy to come a cropper.

The tenth house comes under the rulership of Saturn and Capricorn, both stern taskmasters. The sun sign who feels Saturn pushing him forward must be prepared to work hard, take life seriously, and keep his eye on the material ball. In some horoscopes, this is an onerous destiny, and failure is likely to come simply through lack of heart.

The earth signs all do well in the tenth house, though Virgo and to some extent Taurus may not like the public aspect of it. The water signs, especially Scorpio, may be "dangerous" in the tenth house, wreaking emotional havoc by virtue of the power the tenth house confers on them. For the fire signs, it can be an unbeatable placement—the ideal house for the fiery Aries, Leo, or Sagittarius sun to shine. Air in the tenth is generally neutral, though Gemini might find it a hardship.

Born between 8 and 10 a.m.—SUN IN THE ELEVENTH HOUSE

Like the third and the seventh, the eleventh is one of the so-called "social" houses. The eleventh, which is near the end of the zodiac and therefore more "mature," is social in the broadest sense. It is here we find "friendship"—the awareness of our need for true, binding relationships—among human beings. Many people with the sun in the eleventh house do find that their happiness and success come through friendships, or at least through the willingness to reach out to all.

For certain sun signs, the eleventh house is the ideal "therapy," as it tends to wash away excess egotism and overly material objectives. The "leadership" signs may find their life work within organizations devoted to social causes or philanthropy.

The second and related meaning of the eleventh house is "hopes and wishes." Fanciful-sounding as it seems, this aspect of the eleventh is a great boon to the sun sign that falls into that house. It lends a touch of idealism to the most cynical personality, and a touch of hope to the most downtrodden horoscope. In overall "airy" horoscopes, however, it may make for a tendency to think too much and act too little. Utopia may seem like a real possibility to such a personality, and the whole life may be spent in "hoping" to find it.

Some eleventh-house-sun people seem to have been born under the proverbial "lucky star," benefiting through things that do not seem to benefit other people. There is a touch of Cinderella story in some eleventh-house-sun lives, and the possible reason is that they get back what they give out—love and friendship to all. As with Aquarius, however, eleventh-house-sun people may find their closest relationships are not as close as those of other people. The result of being friend to all also may mean belonging to no one.

Born between 6 and 8 a.m.—SUN IN THE TWELFTH HOUSE

The twelfth is the most "sub" of the subconscious houses, the deepest and darkest of all. For some sun signs, it is the ideal "hiding place"; for others, it is the worst form of solitary confinement. Into the first category fall the introspective water signs. For Cancer, Scorpio, or Pisces, having the sun in this house can literally mean one is a mystic or a contemplative. At the very least, one is extraordinarily sensitive and perceptive. For the earth signs as well as the water signs, the twelfth house—hidden away as it is—is a fairly comfortable place to be, though achievement-oriented Capricorn may suffer. It is the air and especially the fire signs who can feel unduly restrained by the placement of the sun here. Think of it as dropping a burning match into a deep, dark well.

The ancients had little good to say about the twelfth house, and though modern astrologers interpret it quite differently, they too will agree that for the twelfth-house-sun person the real world is not always a bright and cheery place to be. The inner world, and everything that implies, is the province of the twelfth house. Properly understood and integrated into one's life, a twelfth-house placement of the sun can lead to great self-understanding, and an ability to help others understand themselves. Poetry is very "twelfth-house," as is hospital work and work with those who are forced to withdraw from the world, if only temporarily. Coming under the rulership of Pisces and Neptune, the twelfth house presents a problem, but one that is not insoluble. Clarity of thought and a realistic attitude can be cultivated, and the mists of Neptune can be driven away.

5. SUN SIGN CHANGES, 1910–1975

If you were born "on the cusp" (very near the end or the beginning of a sign) you can find out what your sign really is by using the chart that follows. Many people do not realize that the sun does not "change signs" on the same day every year—or, for that matter, at the same time. For this reason the chart of sun sign changes is calculated to the minute.

How to Use the Chart

Locate your year of birth, then the month in which you were born. Let's say you were born in April of 1942. In the box for that month and year you will see

20—Tau
12:30 p.m.

That means if you were born *after* 12:30 p.m. on April 20 in 1942, you are a Taurus. If you were born before that date and time, your sun sign is the preceding one, Aries.

In this chart (as well as in the rising-sign chart) the signs are abbreviated as follows:

Ar = Aries
Tau = Taurus
Gem = Gemini
Can = Cancer
Leo = Leo
Vir = Virgo
Lib = Libra
Sc = Scorpio
Sag = Sagittarius
Cap = Capricorn
Aq = Aquarius
Pis = Pisces

Note: All times given in the sun sign changes chart are Eastern Standard. You must correct for daylight savings time (subtract one hour) and for time zone. For Central Standard Time subtract one hour; for Mountain Standard Time subtract two hours; for Pacific Standard Time subtract three hours.

	1910	1911	1912	1913	1914	1915	1916	1917	1918	1919
Jan	20–Aq 4:59 pm	20–Aq 10:52 pm	20–Aq 4:29 am	20–Aq 10:19 am	20–Aq 4:12 pm	20–Aq 10:00 pm	21–Aq 3:54 am	20–Aq 9:37 am	20–Aq 3:42 pm	19–Aq 10:21 pm
Feb	19–Pis 7:28 am	19–Pis 1:21 pm	19–Pis 6:56 pm	19–Pis 12:45 am	19–Pis 6:38 am	19–Pis 12:23 pm	19–Pis 6:18 pm	19–Pis 12:05 am	19–Pis 5:53 am	19–Pis 11:45 am
Mar	21–Ar 7:03 am	21–Ar 12:55 pm	20–Ar 6:29 pm	21–Ar 12:18 am	21–Ar 6:11 am	21–Ar 11:51 am	20–Ar 7:47 pm	20–Ar 11:37 pm	21–Ar 5:26 am	21–Ar 11:19 am
Apr	20–Tau 6:46 pm	21–Tau 12:36 am	20–Tau 6:12 am	20–Tau 12:03 pm	20–Tau 5:45 pm	20–Tau 11:28 pm	20–Tau 5:25 am	20–Tau 11:17 am	20–Tau 5:06 pm	20–Tau 10:59 pm
May	21–Gem 6:30 pm	22–Gem 12:19 pm	21–Gem 5:27 pm	21–Gem 11:50 am	21–Gem 5:38 pm	21–Gem 11:10 pm	21–Gem 5:06 pm	21–Gem 10:59 pm	21–Gem 4:46 pm	21–Gem 10:39 pm
June	22–Can 2:49 am	22–Can 8:49 am	21–Can 8:09 am	21–Can 8:09 pm	22–Can 1:55 am	22–Can 7:29 am	21–Can 1:25 am	21–Can 7:15 pm	22–Can 1:00 am	22–Can 6:45 am
July	23–Leo 1:43 pm	23–Leo 7:29 pm	23–Leo 7:04 pm	23–Leo 7:04 pm	23–Leo 7:35 pm	23–Leo 6:27 pm	23–Leo 12:21 am	23–Leo 6:08 am	23–Leo 11:52 am	23–Leo 5:45 pm
Aug	23–Vir 8:27 pm	24–Vir 2:13 am	23–Vir 1:48 pm	23–Vir 1:48 pm	23–Vir 12:47 pm	24–Vir 1:16 pm	23–Vir 7:09 am	23–Vir 12:54 pm	23–Vir 6:37 pm	24–Vir 12:28 am
Sept	23–Lib 5:30 pm	23–Lib 11:17 pm	23–Lib 5:08 pm	23–Lib 10:53 am	23–Lib 5:35 pm	24–Lib 10:24 pm	23–Lib 4:15 pm	23–Lib 10:00 pm	24–Lib 3:45 pm	24–Lib 9:35 pm
Oct	24–Sc 2:11 pm	24–Sc 7:59 pm	23–Sc 1:50 pm	23–Sc 7:35 pm	24–Sc 1:18 pm	24–Sc 7:10 pm	23–Sc 12:58 pm	23–Sc 6:44 pm	24–Sc 12:33 am	24–Sc 6:21 am
Nov	22–Sag 11:11 pm	23–Sag 4:57 am	22–Sag 10:48 am	22–Sag 4:36 pm	23–Sag 10:21 pm	23–Sag 4:14 am	22–Sag 9:58 am	22–Sag 3:45 pm	22–Sag 2:38 pm	23–Sag 3:25 am
Dec	22–Cap 12:12 pm	22–Cap 5:53 pm	21–Cap 11:45 pm	22–Cap 5:45 am	22–Cap 11:24 am	22–Cap 5:16 pm	21–Cap 11:45 pm	21–Cap 4:46 am	22–Cap 11:42 am	22–Cap 4:27 pm

	1920	1921	1922	1923	1924	1925	1926	1927	1928	1929
Jan	21-Aq 4:05 am	20-Aq 8:55 am	20-Aq 2:48 pm	20-Aq 8:35 pm	21-Aq 2:29 am	20-Aq 8:20 am	20-Aq 2:13 pm	20-Aq 8:12 pm	21-Aq 1:57 am	20-Aq 7:42 am
Feb	19-Pis 5:29 pm	18-Pis 11:21 pm	19-Pis 5:16 am	19-Pis 11:00 am	19-Pis 4:51 pm	18-Pis 11:43 pm	18-Pis 4:35 am	19-Pis 10:35 am	19-Pis 4:20 pm	18-Pis 10:07 pm
Mar	20-Ar 5:00 pm	20-Ar 10:51 pm	21-Ar 4:49 am	21-Ar 10:29 am	20-Ar 4:20 pm	20-Ar 11:13 pm	21-Ar 4:01 am	21-Ar 11:59 am	20-Ar 3:44 pm	20-Ar 9:35 pm
Apr	20-Tau 4:39 am	20-Tau 10:32 am	20-Tau 4:29 am	20-Tau 10:06 pm	20-Tau 3:59 am	20-Tau 10:51 pm	20-Tau 3:36 pm	20-Tau 9:32 pm	20-Tau 3:17 am	20-Tau 9:11 am
May	21-Gem 4:22 am	21-Gem 10:17 am	21-Gem 9:11 am	22-Gem 9:45 am	21-Gem 3:41 am	21-Gem 10:33 am	21-Gem 3:15 pm	21-Gem 9:08 pm	21-Gem 2:53 am	21-Gem 8:48 am
June	21-Can 12:40pm	21-Can 6:36 pm	22-Can 12:27 am	22-Can 6:03 pm	21-Can 12:noon	21-Can 5:50 pm	21-Can 5:21 am	22-Can 11:30 am	21-Can 11:07 am	21-Can 5:01 pm
July	22-Leo 11:40 pm	23-Leo 5:31 am	23-Leo 11:20 am	23-Leo 5:01 pm	22-Leo 11:58 pm	23-Leo 4:45 am	23-Leo 10:25 am	23-Leo 4:17 am	22-Leo 11:02 pm	23-Leo 3:54 am
Aug	23-Vir 6:22 am	23-Vir 12:15 pm	23-Vir 6:04 pm	23-Vir 11:52 pm	23-Vir 5:48 am	23-Vir 11:33 am	23-Vir 5:14 pm	23-Vir 11:06 am	23-Vir 4:53 am	23-Vir 10:41 am
Sept	23-Lib 3:25 am	23-Lib 11:20 am	23-Lib 5:10 am	23-Lib 9:04 pm	23-Lib 2:58 am	23-Lib 8:43 am	23-Lib 2:25 pm	23-Lib 8:17 pm	23-Lib 2:36 am	23-Lib 7:52 am
Oct	23-Sc 12:31 pm	23-Sc 6:03 pm	23-Sc 11:53 am	24-Sc 5:51 am	23-Sc 11:44 am	23-Sc 5:31 pm	23-Sc 11:18 pm	24-Sc 5:07 am	23-Sc 10:55 am	23-Sc 4:41 pm
Nov	22-Sag 9:15 am	22-Sag 3:21 pm	22-Sag 8:55 pm	23-Sag 2:54 am	22-Sag 8:46 am	22-Sag 2:36 pm	22-Sag 8:28 pm	23-Sag 2:14 am	22-Sag 8:00 am	22-Sag 1:48 pm
Dec	21-Cap 10:17 pm	22-Cap 4:08 am	22-Cap 9:57 pm	22-Cap 3:53 pm	21-Cap 10:45 pm	22-Cap 3:37 am	22-Cap 9:34 am	22-cap 3:18 pm	21-Cap 9:04 pm	22-Cap 2:53 am

	1930	1931	1932	1933	1934	1935	1936	1937	1938	1939
Jan	20–Aq 1:33 pm	21–Aq 7:18 pm	20–Aq 1:07 pm	20–Aq 6:53 pm	20–Aq 10:37 am	20–Aq 6:29 pm	21–Aq 12:12am	20–Aq 6:01 am	20–Aq 11:59 am	20–Aq 5:51 pm
Feb	19–Pis 4:00 am	19–Pis 9:06 am	19–Pis 3:29 pm	19–Pis 9:16 pm	19–Pis 3:02 am	19–Pis 8:52 am	19–Pis 2:33 pm	18–Pis 3:21 pm	19–Pis 2:20 am	19–Pis 8:10 pm
Mar	21–Ar 3:30 am	21–Ar 9:40 am	20–Ar 2:54 pm	21–Ar 8:43 pm	21–Ar 2:28 am	21–Ar 8:19 am	20–Ar 1:58 pm	20–Ar 7:45 pm	21–Ar 1:43 am	21–Ar 7:29 am
Apr	20–Tau 3:06 pm	20–Tau 8:40 pm	20–Tau 2:28 am	20–Tau 8:19 am	20–Tau 2:00 pm	20–Tau 7:50 pm	20–Tau 1:31 am	20–Tau 7:20 am	20–Tau 1:15 pm	20–Tau 6:55 pm
May	21–Gem 2:42 pm	21–Gem 8:15 pm	21–Gem 2:07 am	21–Gem 7:57 am	21–Gem 1:35 pm	21–Gem 7:25 pm	21–Gem 1:08 am	21–Gem 6:57 am	21–Gem 12:51 pm	21–Gem 6:27 pm
June	21–Can 11:53 pm	21–Can 4:28 am	21–Can 10:23 am	21–Can 4:12 pm	21–Can 9:48 pm	22–Can 3:32 am	21–Can 9:22 am	21–Can 3:12 pm	21–Can 9:04 pm	22–Can 2:40 am
July	23–Leo 10:42 am	23–Leo 3:21 pm	22–Leo 9:18 pm	23–Leo 3:06 am	23–Leo 8:42 am	23–Leo 2:33 pm	22–Leo 8:18 am	23–Leo 2:07 am	23–Leo 7:57 am	23–Leo 1:37 pm
Aug	23–Vir 4:27 pm	23–Vir 10:10 pm	23–Vir 4:06 am	23–Vir 9:53 am	23–Vir 3:32 pm	23–Vir 9:24 pm	23–Vir 3:11 am	23–Vir 8:58 am	23–Vir 2:46 pm	23–Vir 8:31 pm
Sept	23–Lib 1:35 pm	23–Lib 7:23 pm	23–Lib 1:16 am	23–Lib 7:01 am	23–Lib 10:45 am	24–Lib 6:38 pm	23–Lib 12:26 am	23–Lib 6:13 am	23–Lib 12:noon	23–Lib 5:50 pm
Oct	23–Sc 11:25 pm	24–Sc 4:15 am	23–Sc 10:04 am	23–Sc 3:48 pm	23–Sc 9:35 pm	24–Sc 3:29 am	23–Sc 10:18 am	23–Sc 3:06 pm	23–Sc 8:54 pm	24–Sc 2:46 am
Nov	22–Sag 7:34 pm	23–Sag 1:25 pm	22–Sag 7:10 am	22–Sag 10:53 am	22–Sag 6:44 pm	23–Sag 12:35 am	22–Sag 6:25 pm	22–Sag 12:17 pm	22–Sag 6:06 pm	22–Sag 11:59 pm
Dec	22–Cap 8:40 am	22–Cap 2:30 pm	21–Cap 8:14 pm	22–Cap 1:58 am	22–Cap 5:49 pm	22–Cap 1:37 pm	21–Cap 7:27 pm	22–Cap 1:22 am	22–Cap 7:13 am	22–Cap 1:05 pm

	1940	1941	1942	1943	1944	1945	1946	1947	1948
Jan	20–Aq, 11:44 pm	20–Aq, 5:34 am	20–Aq, 11:16 am	20–Aq, 5:20 pm	20–Aq, 11:09 pm	20–Aq, 4:55 am	20–Aq, 10:44 am	20–Aq, 4:23 pm	20–Aq, 10:18 pm
Feb	19–Pis, 2:04 pm	18–Pis, 7:59 pm	19–Pis, 1:39 am	19–Pis, 7:41 am	19–Pis, 1:28 pm	18–Pis, 7:15 pm	19–Pis, 1:10 am	19–Pis, 6:53 am	19–Pis, 12:37 pm
Mar	20–Ar, 1:24 pm	20–Ar, 7:21 pm	21–Ar, 1:03 am	21–Ar, 7:03 am	21–Ar, 12:49 pm	20–Ar, 6:38 pm	21–Ar, 12:34 am	21–Ar, 6:13 am	20–Ar, 11:57 am
Apr	20–Tau, 12:51 am	20–Tau, 6:51 am	20–Tau, 12:30 pm	20–Tau, 6:32 pm	20–Tau, 12:18 am	20–Tau, 6:08 am	20–Tau, 12:03 pm	20–Tau, 5:40 pm	20–Tau, 11:25 pm
May	21–Gem, 12:23 am	21–Gem, 6:23 am	21–Gem, 12:01 pm	21–Gem, 6:03 pm	20–Gem, 11:51 pm	22–Gem, 5:41 am	21–Gem, 11:34 am	21–Gem, 5:04 pm	20–Gem, 10:58 pm
June	21–Can, 8:37 am	21–Can, 2:33 pm	21–Can, 8:08 pm	22–Can, 2:13 am	21–Can, 9:03 am	21–Can, 1:52 pm	21–Can, 7:45 pm	22–Can, 1:19 am	21–Can, 7:11 am
July	22–Leo, 7:34 pm	23–Leo, 1:26 am	23–Leo, 6:59 am	23–Leo, 1:05 pm	22–Leo, 6:55 pm	23–Leo, 12:48 am	23–Leo, 6:37 am	23–Leo, 12:12 pm	22–Leo, 6:06 pm
Aug	23–Vir, 2:21 am	23–Vir, 8:30 am	23–Vir, 1:50 pm	23–Vir, 7:55 pm	23–Vir, 1:47 am	23–Vir, 7:36 am	23–Vir, 1:23 pm	23–Vir, 7:09 pm	23–Vir, 1:03 am
Sept	22–Lib, 11:46 pm	23–Lib, 5:33 am	23–Lib, 11:10 am	23–Lib, 5:12 pm	22–Lib, 11:02 pm	23–Lib, 4:50 am	23–Lib, 10:41 am	23–Lib, 4:29 pm	22–Lib, 10:22 pm
Oct	23–Sc, 8:39 am	23–Sc, 2:22 pm	22–Sc, 8:01 pm	24–Sc, 2:09 am	23–Sc, 7:57 am	23–Sc, 1:45 pm	23–Sc, 7:37 pm	24–Sc, 1:27 am	23–Sc, 7:19 am
Nov	22–Sag, 5:49 am	22–Sag, 11:38 am	22–Sag, 5:23 pm	22–Sag, 11:22 pm	22–Sag, 5:09 am	22–Sag, 10:56 am	22–Sag, 4:47 pm	22–Sag, 10:38 pm	22–Sag, 4:29 am
Dec	21–Cap, 6:55 pm	22–Cap, 12:44 am	22–Cap, 6:31 am	22–Cap, 12:30 pm	21–Cap, 6:15 pm	22–Cap, 12:04 am	22–Cap, 5:54 am	22–Cap, 11:44 am	21–Cap, 5:23 pm

	1949	1950	1951	1952	1953	1954	1955	1956	1957
Jan	20—Aq 4:11 am	20—Aq 10:00 am	20—Aq 3:53 pm	20—Aq 9:38 pm	20—Aq 3:22 am	20—Aq 9:14 am	20—Aq 3:03 pm	20—Aq 8:49 pm	20—Aq 2:43 am
Feb	18—Pis 6:27 pm	19—Pis 12:16 am	19—Pis 6:10 am	19—Pis 11:57 am	18—Pis 5:41 pm	19—Pis 11:33 pm	19—Pis 5:19 am	19—Pis 11:05 am	18—Pis 5:01 pm
Mar	20—Ar 5:49 pm	20—Ar 11:30 pm	21—Ar 5:26 am	20—Ar 11:14 am	20—Ar 5:01 pm	20—Ar 10:54 pm	21—Ar 4:36 am	20—Ar 10:21 am	20—Ar 4:17 pm
Apr	20—Tau 5:18 am	20—Tau 11:00 am	20—Tau 4:49 pm	20—Tau 10:37 pm	20—Tau 4:26 am	20—Tau 10:20 am	20—Tau 3:58 pm	19—Tau 9:44 pm	20—Tau 3:45 am
May	21—Gem 4:51 am	21—Gem 10:27 am	21—Gem 4:15 pm	21—Gem 10:04 pm	21—Gem 3:53 am	21—Gem 9:48 am	21—Gem 3:25 pm	20—Gem 9:13 pm	21—Gem 3:09 am
June	21—Can 1:03 pm	21—Can 6:37 pm	22—Can 12:25 am	21—Can 6:13 am	21—Can 12:noon	21—Can 5:55 pm	21—Can 11:32 pm	21—Can 5:24 am	21—Can 11:21 am
July	22—Leo 1:58 pm	23—Leo 5:30 pm	23—Leo 11:29 am	22—Leo 5:05 pm	22—Leo 10:53 pm	23—Leo 4:45 am	23—Leo 10:25 am	22—Leo 4:20 pm	22—Leo 10:13 pm
Aug	23—Vir 6:49 pm	23—Vir 12:24 pm	23—Vir 6:22 pm	23—Vir 12:03 am	23—Vir 5:46 am	23—Vir 11:37 am	23—Vir 5:19 pm	22—Vir 11:15 pm	23—Vir 5:07 am
Sept	23—Lib 4:05 am	23—Lib 9:44 am	23—Lib 3:38 pm	22—Lib 9:24 pm	23—Lib 3:07 am	23—Lib 8:56 am	23—Lib 2:42 pm	22—Lib 8:30 pm	23—Lib 2:27 am
Oct	23—Sc 1:04 pm	23—Sc 6:48 pm	23—Sc 12:37 am	23—Sc 6:22 am	23—Sc 12:07 pm	23—Sc 5:58 pm	23—Sc 11:44 pm	23—Sc 5:35 am	23—Sc 11:33 am
Nov	22—Sag 10:17 am	22—Sag 4:03 pm	22—Sag 9:52 pm	22—Sag 3:36 am	22—Sag 9:23 pm	22—Sag 3:14 pm	22—Sag 9:02 pm	22—Sag 2:51 am	22—Sag 8:45 am
Dec	21—Cap 11:24 am	22—Cap 5:14 am	22—Cap 11:01 am	21—Cap 4:44 pm	21—Cap 10:22 pm	22—Cap 4:25 am	22—Cap 10:12 am	21—Cap 4:00 pm	21—Cap 9:49 pm

	1958	1959	1960	1961	1962	1963	1964	1965	1966
Jan	20–Aq 2:20 pm	20–Aq 2:20 pm	20–Aq 8:11 pm	20–Aq 2:02 am	20–Aq 7:49 am	20–Aq 1:55 pm	19–Aq 7:43 pm	20–Aq 1:30 am	20–Aq 8:21 am
Feb	18–Pis 10:49 pm	19–Pis 4:38 pm	19–Pis 10:26 pm	18–Pis 6:27 pm	18–Pis 10:16 pm	19–Pis 4:09 pm	19–Pis 10:25 am	18–Pis 3:49 pm	18–Pis 9:39 pm
Mar	20–Ar 10:06 pm	21–Ar 3:55 am	20–Ar 9:43 am	20–Ar 5:27 am	20–Ar 9:30 pm	21–Ar 3:20 am	20–Ar 9:43 am	20–Ar 3:05 pm	20–Ar 8:53 pm
Apr	20–Tau 9:28 am	20–Tau 3:17 pm	20–Tau 10:06 pm	20–Tau 2:33 am	20–Tau 8:51 am	20–Tau 2:37 pm	19–Tau 9:00 pm	20–Tau 2:27 am	20–Tau 8:12 am
May	21–Gem 8:52 am	21–Gem 2:38 pm	20–Gem 8:33 pm	21–Gem 1:51 am	21–Gem 8:17 am	21–Gem 1:59 pm	20–Gem 8:33 pm	21–Gem 1:27 am	21–Gem 7:33 am
June	21–Can 4:57 pm	21–Can 10:50 pm	21–Can 4:43 am	21–Can 10:12 am	21–Can 4:24 pm	21–Can 11:04 pm	21–Can 4:43 am	21–Can 9:56 am	21–Can 3:33 pm
July	23–Leo 3:51 am	23–Leo 9:45 am	22–Leo 5:38 pm	22–Leo 9:12 pm	23–Leo 3:19 am	23–Leo 9:00 am	22–Leo 3:38 pm	22–Leo 8:49 pm	23–Leo 2:24 am
Aug	23–Vir 10:47 am	23–Vir 4:44 pm	22–Vir 10:35 pm	23–Vir 3:46 am	23–Vir 10:13 am	23–Vir 3:58 pm	22–Vir 10:35 pm	23–Vir 3:43 am	23–Vir 9:18 am
Sept	23–Lib 5:10 am	23–Lib 2:09 pm	22–Lib 8:00 pm	23–Lib 1:26 am	23–Lib 7:35 am	23–Lib 1:24 pm	22–Lib 8:00 pm	23–Lib 1:06 am	23–Lib 6:43 am
Oct	23–Sc 5:12 am	23–Sc 11:12 pm	23–Sc 5:03 am	23–Sc 10:46 am	23–Sc 4:41 pm	23–Sc 11:30 pm	23–Sc 5:03 am	23–Sc 10:11 am	23–Sc 3:52 pm
Nov	22–Sag 2:30 pm	22–Sag 8:23 pm	22–Sag 2:19 am	22–Sag 8:10 am	22–Sag 2:02 pm	22–Sag 7:50 pm	22–Sag 2:19 am	22–Sag 7:30 am	22–Sag 1:15 pm
Dec	22–Cap 3:40 am	22–Cap 9:35 am	21–Cap 5:27 pm	21–Cap 9:25 pm	22–Cap 3:15 am	22–Cap 9:02 am	21–Cap 3:27 pm	21–Cap 8:41 pm	22–Cap 2:29 pm

	1967	1968	1969	1970	1971	1972	1973	1974	1975
Jan	20-Aq 1:05 pm	20-Aq 6:54 pm	20-Aq 12:30 am	20-Aq 6:25 am	20-Aq 12:14 pm	20-Aq 6:00 pm	19-Aq 11:49 pm	20-Aq 5:47 am	20-Aq 11:37 am
Feb	19-Pis 3:25 am	19-Pis 9:11 am	18-Pis 2:47 pm	18-Pis 8:43 pm	19-Pis 2:28 am	19-Pis 8:12am	18-Pis 2:02 pm	18-Pis 8:00 pm	19-Pis 1:51 am
Mar	21-Ar 2:37 am	20-Ar 8:22 am	20-Ar 2:08 pm	20-Ar 7:59 pm	21-Ar 1:28 am	20-Ar 7:22 am	20-Ar 1:13 pm	20-Ar 7:08 pm	21-Ar 12:58 am
Apr	20-Tau 1:56 am	19-Tau 7:42 pm	20-Tau 1:18 am	20-Tau 5:16 am	20-Tau 12:54 pm	19-Tau 6:38 pm	20-Tau 12:31 am	20-Tau 5:19 am	20-Tau 12:08 pm
May	21-Gem 1:19 pm	20-Gem 7:07 pm	21-Gem 12:41 am	21-Gem 6:32 am	21-Gem 12:16 pm	20-Gem 6:00 pm	20-Gem 11:54 pm	21-Gem 5:37 am	21-Gem 1:25 pm
June	21-Can 4:23 pm	21-Can 1:13 am	21-Can 6:55 am	21-Can 2:43 pm	21-Can 8:21 pm	21-Can 2:07 am	21-Can 8:01 am	21-Can 1:38 pm	21-Can 7:27 pm
July	23-Leo 8:16 am	22-Leo 2:13 pm	22-Leo 8:05 pm	23-Leo 1:38 am	23-Leo 7:15 am	22-Leo 1:03 pm	22-Leo 6:56 pm	23-Leo 12:30 am	23-Leo 7:23 am
Aug	23-Vir 3:13 pm	22-Vir 9:52 pm	23-Vir 2:35 am	23-Vir 6:35 am	23-Vir 2:16 pm	22-Vir 8:04 pm	23-Vir 1:55 am	23-Vir 7:29 am	23-Vir 1:24 pm
Sept	23-Lib 12:38 pm	22-Lib 6:26 pm	23-Lib 12:07 am	23-Lib 5:59 am	23-Lib 11:47 am	22-Lib 5:34 pm	22-Lib 11:22 pm	23-Lib 4:59 am	23-Lib 10:56 am
Oct	23-Sc 9:44 pm	23-Sc 1:30 am	23-Sc 9:03 am	23-Sc 3:05 pm	22-Sc 8:53 pm	23-Sc 2:42 am	23-Sc 8:31 am	23-Sc 2:12 pm	23-Sc 8:07 pm
Nov	22-Sag 7:05 pm	22-Sag 12:59 am	22-Sag 6:23 am	22-Sag 12:25 pm	22-Sag 6:15 pm	22-Sag 12:04 am	22-Sag 5:55 am	22-Sag 11:39 am	22-Sag 5:32 pm
Dec	22-Cap 8:17 am	21-Cap 2:00 pm	21-Cap 7:44 pm	22-Cap 1:36 am	22-Cap 5:26 am	21-Cap 1:14 pm	21-Cap 7:09 pm	22-Cap 12:57 am	22-Cap 7:47 am

6. FIND YOUR RISING SIGN

It is easier than many people think to find out your rising sign. One reason is that it is based on "universal" or "sidereal" time—the measure used in space travel. To ascertain your rising sign, look through the following chart and locate the birthdate nearest your birth date; look across and locate the time nearest your birth time. Remember that if daylight saving time was in effect at your birth, you must subtract one hour from the time stated on your birth certificate. In the section for your date and time, you will find an abbreviation for the sign that was rising when you were born. For instance, if your birthdate is June 12 at 9:30 a.m., your rising sign is Leo; if you were born on the same date at 9:30 p.m., your rising sign is Capricorn.

You will notice that the *year* you were born does not affect your rising sign. However, the geographical latitude does. These tables are calculated for the middle latitudes of the United States. If you were born far to the south, it is wise to look at the sign that *follows* your rising sign as well. If you were born far to the north, check out the *previous* sign.

Rising Signs—A.M. Births

	1 AM	2 AM	3 AM	4 AM	5 AM	6 AM	7 AM	8 AM	9 AM	10 AM	11 AM	12 NOON
Jan 1	Lib	Sc	Sc	Sc	Sag	Sag	Cap	Cap	Aq	Aq	Pis	Ar
Jan 9	Lib	Sc	Sc	Sag	Sag	Sag	Cap	Cap	Aq	Pis	Ar	Tau
Jan 17	Sc	Sc	Sc	Sag	Sag	Cap	Cap	Aq	Aq	Pis	Ar	Tau
Jan 25	Sc	Sc	Sag	Sag	Sag	Cap	Cap	Aq	Pis	Ar	Tau	Tau
Feb 2	Sc	Sc	Sag	Sag	Cap	Cap	Aq	Pis	Pis	Ar	Tau	Gem
Feb 10	Sc	Sag	Sag	Sag	Cap	Cap	Aq	Pis	Ar	Tau	Tau	Gem
Feb 18	Sc	Sag	Sag	Cap	Cap	Aq	Pis	Pis	Ar	Tau	Gem	Gem
Feb 26	Sag	Sag	Sag	Cap	Aq	Aq	Pis	Ar	Tau	Tau	Gem	Gem
Mar 6	Sag	Sag	Cap	Cap	Aq	Pis	Pis	Ar	Tau	Gem	Gem	Cap
Mar 14	Sag	Cap	Cap	Aq	Aq	Pis	Ar	Tau	Tau	Gem	Gem	Can
Mar 22	Sag	Cap	Cap	Aq	Pis	Ar	Ar	Tau	Gem	Gem	Can	Can
Mar 30	Cap	Cap	Aq	Pis	Pis	Ar	Tau	Tau	Gem	Can	Can	Can
Apr 7	Cap	Cap	Aq	Pis	Ar	Ar	Tau	Gem	Gem	Can	Can	Leo
Apr 14	Cap	Aq	Aq	Pis	Ar	Tau	Tau	Gem	Gem	Can	Can	Leo
Apr 22	Cap	Aq	Pis	Ar	Ar	Tau	Gem	Gem	Gem	Can	Leo	Leo
Apr 30	Aq	Aq	Pis	Ar	Tau	Tau	Gem	Can	Can	Can	Leo	Leo
May 8	Aq	Pis	Ar	Ar	Tau	Gem	Gem	Can	Can	Leo	Leo	Leo
May 16	Aq	Pis	Ar	Tau	Gem	Gem	Can	Can	Can	Leo	Leo	Vir
May 24	Pis	Ar	Ar	Tau	Gem	Gem	Can	Can	Leo	Leo	Leo	Vir
June 1	Pis	Ar	Tau	Gem	Gem	Can	Can	Can	Leo	Leo	Vir	Vir
June 9	Ar	Ar	Tau	Gem	Gem	Can	Can	Leo	Leo	Leo	Vir	Vir
June 17	Ar	Tau	Gem	Gem	Can	Can	Can	Leo	Leo	Vir	Vir	Vir
June 25	Tau	Tau	Gem	Gem	Can	Can	Leo	Leo	Leo	Vir	Vir	Lib
July 3	Tau	Gem	Gem	Can	Can	Can	Leo	Leo	Vir	Vir	Vir	Lib
July 11	Tau	Gem	Gem	Can	Can	Leo	Leo	Leo	Vir	Vir	Lib	Lib
July 18	Gem	Gem	Can	Can	Can	Leo	Leo	Vir	Vir	Vir	Lib	Lib
July 26	Gem	Gem	Can	Can	Leo	Leo	Vir	Vir	Vir	Lib	Lib	Lib
Aug 3	Gem	Can	Can	Can	Leo	Leo	Vir	Vir	Vir	Lib	Lib	Sc
Aug 11	Gem	Can	Can	Leo	Leo	Leo	Vir	Vir	Lib	Lib	Lib	Sc
Aug 18	Can	Can	Can	Leo	Leo	Vir	Vir	Vir	Lib	Lib	Sc	Sc
Aug 27	Can	Can	Leo	Leo	Leo	Vir	Vir	Lib	Lib	Lib	Sc	Sc
Sept 4	Can	Can	Leo	Leo	Leo	Vir	Vir	Vir	Lib	Lib	Sc	Sc
Sept 12	Can	Leo	Leo	Leo	Vir	Vir	Lib	Lib	Lib	Sc	Sc	Sag
Sept 30	Leo	Leo	Leo	Vir	Vir	Vir	Lib	Lib	Sc	Sc	Sc	Sag
Sept 28	Leo	Leo	Leo	Vir	Vir	Lib	Lib	Lib	Sc	Sc	Sag	Sag
Oct 6	Leo	Leo	Vir	Vir	Vir	Lib	Lib	Sc	Sc	Sc	Sag	Sag
Oct 14	Leo	Vir	Vir	Vir	Lib	Lib	Lib	Sc	Sc	Sag	Sag	Cap
Oct 22	Leo	Vir	Vir	Lib	Lib	Lib	Sc	Sc	Sc	Sag	Sag	Cap
Oct 30	Vir	Vir	Vir	Lib	Lib	Sc	Sc	Sc	Sag	Sag	Cap	Cap
Nov 7	Vir	Vir	Lib	Lib	Lib	Sc	Sc	Sc	Sag	Sag	Cap	Cap
Nov 15	Vir	Vir	Lib	Lib	Sc	Sc	Sc	Sag	Sag	Cap	Cap	Aq
Nov 23	Vir	Lib	Lib	Lib	Sc	Sc	Sag	Sag	Sag	Cap	Cap	Aq
Dec 1	Vir	Lib	Lib	Sc	Sc	Sc	Sag	Sag	Cap	Cap	Aq	Aq
Dec 9	Lib	Lib	Lib	Sc	Sc	Sag	Sag	Sag	Cap	Cap	Aq	Pis
Dec 18	Lib	Lib	Sc	Sc	Sc	Sag	Sag	Cap	Cap	Aq	Aq	Pis
Dec 28	Lib	Lib	Sc	Sc	Sag	Sag	Sag	Cap	Aq	Aq	Pis	Ar

Rising Signs—P.M. Births

	1 PM	2 PM	3 PM	4 PM	5 PM	6 PM	7 PM	8 PM	9 PM	10 PM	11 PM	12 MIDNIGHT
Jan 1	Tau	Gem	Gem	Can	Can	Can	Leo	Leo	Vir	Vir	Vir	Lib
Jan 9	Tau	Gem	Gem	Can	Can	Leo	Leo	Leo	Vir	Vir	Vir	Lib
Jan 17	Gem	Gem	Can	Can	Can	Leo	Leo	Vir	Vir	Vir	Lib	Lib
Jan 25	Gem	Gem	Can	Can	Leo	Leo	Leo	Vir	Vir	Lib	Lib	Lib
Feb 2	Gem	Can	Can	Can	Leo	Leo	Vir	Vir	Vir	Lib	Lib	Sc
Feb 10	Gem	Can	Can	Leo	Leo	Leo	Vir	Vir	Lib	Lib	Lib	Sc
Feb 18	Can	Can	Can	Leo	Leo	Vir	Vir	Vir	Lib	Lib	Sc	Sc
Feb 26	Can	Can	Leo	Leo	Leo	Vir	Vir	Lib	Lib	Lib	Sc	Sc
Mar 6	Can	Leo	Leo	Leo	Vir	Vir	Vir	Lib	Lib	Sc	Sc	Sc
Mar 14	Can	Leo	Leo	Vir	Vir	Vir	Lib	Lib	Lib	Sc	Sc	Sag
Mar 22	Leo	Leo	Leo	Vir	Vir	Lib	Lib	Lib	Sc	Sc	Sc	Sag
Mar 30	Leo	Leo	Vir	Vir	Vir	Lib	Lib	Sc	Sc	Sc	Sag	Sag
Apr 7	Leo	Leo	Vir	Vir	Lib	Lib	Lib	Sc	Sc	Sc	Sag	Sag
Apr 14	Leo	Vir	Vir	Vir	Lib	Lib	Sc	Sc	Sc	Sag	Sag	Cap
Apr 22	Leo	Vir	Vir	Lib	Lib	Lib	Sc	Sc	Sc	Sag	Sag	Cap
Apr 30	Vir	Vir	Vir	Lib	Lib	Sc	Sc	Sc	Sag	Sag	Cap	Cap
May 8	Vir	Vir	Lib	Lib	Lib	Sc	Sc	Sag	Sag	Sag	Cap	Cap
May 16	Vir	Vir	Lib	Lib	Sc	Sc	Sc	Sag	Sag	Cap	Cap	Aq
May 24	Vir	Lib	Lib	Lib	Sc	Sc	Sag	Sag	Sag	Cap	Cap	Aq
June 1	Vir	Lib	Lib	Sc	Sc	Sc	Sag	Sag	Cap	Cap	Aq	Aq
June 9	Lib	Lib	Lib	Sc	Sc	Sag	Sag	Sag	Cap	Cap	Aq	Pis
June 17	Lib	Lib	Sc	Sc	Sc	Sag	Sag	Cap	Cap	Aq	Aq	Pis
June 25	Lib	Lib	Sc	Sc	Sag	Sag	Sag	Cap	Cap	Aq	Pis	Ar
July 3	Lib	Sc	Sc	Sc	Sag	Sag	Cap	Cap	Aq	Aq	Pis	Ar
July 11	Lib	Sc	Sc	Sag	Sag	Sag	Cap	Cap	Aq	Pis	Ar	Tau
July 18	Sc	Sc	Sc	Sag	Sag	Cap	Cap	Aq	Aq	Pis	Ar	Tau
July 26	Sc	Sc	Sag	Sag	Sag	Cap	Cap	Aq	Pis	Ar	Tau	Tau
Aug 3	Sc	Sc	Sag	Sag	Cap	Cap	Aq	Aq	Pis	Ar	Tau	Gem
Aug 11	Sc	Sag	Sag	Sag	Cap	Cap	Aq	Pis	Ar	Tau	Tau	Gem
Aug 18	Sc	Sag	Sag	Cap	Cap	Aq	Pis	Pis	Ar	Tau	Gem	Gem
Aug 27	Sag	Sag	Sag	Cap	Cap	Aq	Pis	Ar	Tau	Tau	Gem	Gem
Sept 4	Sag	Sag	Cap	Cap	Aq	Pis	Pis	Ar	Tau	Gem	Gem	Can
Sept 12	Sag	Sag	Cap	Aq	Aq	Pis	Ar	Tau	Tau	Gem	Gem	Can
Sept 20	Sag	Cap	Cap	Aq	Pis	Pis	Ar	Tau	Gem	Gem	Can	Can
Sept 28	Cap	Cap	Aq	Aq	Pis	Ar	Tau	Tau	Gem	Gem	Can	Can
Oct 6	Cap	Cap	Aq	Pis	Ar	Ar	Tau	Gem	Gem	Can	Can	Leo
Oct 14	Cap	Aq	Aq	Pis	Ar	Tau	Tau	Gem	Gem	Can	Can	Leo
Oct 22	Cap	Aq	Pis	Ar	Ar	Tau	Gem	Gem	Can	Can	Leo	Leo
Oct 30	Aq	Aq	Pis	Ar	Tau	Tau	Gem	Can	Can	Can	Leo	Leo
Nov 7	Aq	Aq	Pis	Ar	Tau	Tau	Gem	Can	Can	Can	Leo	Leo
Nov 15	Aq	Pis	Ar	Tau	Gem	Gem	Can	Can	Can	Leo	Leo	Vir
Nov 23	Pis	Ar	Ar	Tau	Gem	Gem	Can	Can	Leo	Leo	Leo	Vir
Dec 1	Pis	Ar	Tau	Gem	Gem	Can	Can	Can	Leo	Leo	Vir	Vir
Dec 9	Ar	Tau	Tau	Gem	Gem	Can	Can	Leo	Leo	Leo	Vir	Vir
Dec 18	Ar	Tau	Gem	Gem	Can	Can	Can	Leo	Leo	Vir	Vir	Vir
Dec 28	Tau	Tau	Gem	Gem	Can	Can	Leo	Leo	Vir	Vir	Vir	Lib

7. THE PLANETS: KEY TO COMPATIBILITY

In popular astrology there is so much emphasis on the signs of the zodiac that it is easy to forget the planets, which are in fact the prime movers of personality. In the "occult" tradition that underlies all astrological thought, the human being is seen as a microcosm of our solar system—that is, a miniature of the macrocosm of our universe. In medical astrology each part of the body is "ruled" by a different planet; in natal astrology certain personality traits are ascribed to certain planets. It is from the planets that the signs of the zodiac receive their particular individuality—which is why they are the key to interpersonal compatibility. The source of the "energy" we give off, the planets determine how that energy interacts with that of others. Some planetary combinations signal clash and conflict; others a neutralizing of energy; still others a sparky but interesting friction, or a beautiful synergy.

Which Planets Rule Which Signs?

In our solar system there are at present ten known "planets." (Astrological terminology takes the liberty of calling the sun and moon "planets" in the sense that they also rule or correspond to specific signs of the zodiac.) Since there are twelve signs of the zodiac, two planets—Mercury and Venus—rule two signs each. These are the rulership "assignments" most modern astrologers give the planets:

Sun	Leo
Moon	Cancer
Mercury	Gemini and Virgo
Venus	Taurus and Libra
Mars	Aries
Jupiter	Sagittarius
Saturn	Capricorn
Uranus	Aquarius
Neptune	Pisces
Pluto	Scorpio

People sometimes point to an apparent "flaw" in the planet-assignment system: What did astrologers do before the discovery of the "modern" planets—Uranus, Neptune, and Pluto? Early astrologers indeed knew of only seven planets, which means certain signs have both "traditional" and "modern" rulers.

	Ancient Ruler	Modern Ruler
Aquarius	Saturn	Uranus
Pisces	Jupiter	Neptune
Scorpio	Mars	Pluto

Some astrologers believe there are still planets to come, and that someday we'll have a neat twelve-planet, twelve-sign arrangement. However, planetary assignments are far from arbitrary. As a matter of fact, when looking at your own compatibility pattern in this chapter, it is wise to look at *both* your ancient and your modern ruler if you are a Scorpio, an Aquarian, or a Pisces. You probably will find "parts of yourself" in each place.

If you think about it, you realize our language is peppered with planet-derived descriptions of moods and personality types. One can be said to have a "sunny" disposition; "lunatics" were once thought to be moon-struck to the ultimate degree; you march to "martial" music; "jovial" people are often ruled by Jove, the Latin name for Jupiter; "mercurial" types move fast and are hard to pin down, like the metal itself.

Astrology has received a lot of good press in recent years in the area of planetary influences on personality. A French statistician, Michel Gaquelin, and his wife undertook a research project designed to "disprove" astrology. Instead, their research took them in a surprisingly positive direction. This scientific team now claim they have statistical proof that certain planets—when prominently placed in the horoscope—are a definite factor in the careers of many famous people. In their book, *Your Personality and the Planets*, the Gaquelins delineate the character of a number of famous individuals with respect to their dominant planet or planets. The list ranges from "Jupiterian" Franklin Delano Roosevelt to "Saturnine" Richard Nixon, and includes people like successful businessman Jean Paul Getty (Saturn), Brigitte Bardot (Venus), Mohammad Ali (Mars), George Bernard Shaw (moon), Adolph Hitler (Jupiter), and Elvis Presley (Jupiter).

While the Gaquelins based their conclusions on *only* the planets and their placement in the horoscope and *not* on the zodiac signs, for our purposes here your dominant planet will be the one that rules your sun sign. Keep in mind, however, that the total horoscope is a mixture of planetary influences. While the ruler of your sun sign is generally the most important, in some cases the planet that rules your rising sign can have a great or almost equal influence on your personality and hence on your compatibility with others. If you know the time of day you were born, use the table on pages 69 to 70 to determine your rising sign, and read those sections of this chapter as well.

The Cast of Characters

When dealing with symbolic concepts like the influence of the planets it is sometimes most productive to use the "personification" technique. In the dialogues that follow, each planet will "speak" according to its nature. Here are some clues to help you visualize the characters in these mini-dramas designed to illustrate compatibility. Like the signs, each planet has a "sex." At first you may find it confusing to think of yourself, as defined by your ruling planet, as a person of the opposite sex. Far from being a confusion, this factor has great importance in the assessment of compatibility, so it is wise to make the effort to think of yourself in a different sex role.

Sun: A prepossessing male who can exert great authority and often thinks of himself as the center of the universe. He is not particularly insightful, however, and his charm often stems from his "innocence."

Moon: A warm and sympathetic lady who sometimes overreacts because she feels all sensations and emotions so acutely—both her own and those of other people. She would take care of you if she could.

Mercury: A complex hermaphrodite with several signs as well as sides to his/her character. Clever and often witty, Mercury can be evasive, exacting, entertaining, and exasperating—sometimes all at the same time.

Venus: A lovely lady who loves the more beautiful things in this world. Peace and harmony are her true goals, and she will have them if she can—sometimes by passive force, sometimes by smiling stubbornness. A sybarite, she can surprise with her healthy desires—though she is fastidious.

Mars: A virile young man with winning on his mind. He talks tough sometimes, which can make you overlook his instinctive generosity. Impatient to a fault, he sometimes quits the field before the race is over.

Jupiter: A jovial, expansive character who sometimes acts a little like Daddy Warbucks. Capable of magnificent gestures as well as startling frankness, he is generally so good-humored that people seek his company. He hates to be alone.

Saturn: A terribly hardworking, serious fellow, he seemed old at birth. Patience, thrift, stick-to-itiveness, and punctuality can be numbered among his virtues; sadness, rigidity, and mistrust can bring both him and others down.

Uranus: A hermaphrodite with a definite slant toward the male polarity. Ingenious and sometimes even brilliant, Uranus can be quite unpredictable, and hence unsettling to more settled types. In his life there's always something new.

Neptune: A mysterious older woman who seems to know the secrets of the universe. She can charm you with her hazy, beautiful thoughts and uplift you with her idealism. The problem is: Does she have substance?

Pluto: A powerful, determined male who can be a bit of an enigma. You feel his force rather than see it, because he often wears a mask of subtle self-control. Don't mess with him, however, if you value your life and your sanity.

Each of the following sections sets up a situation which revolves around one of the planets. That planet asks a question or makes a statement to which all of the other planets must respond. Though some of the situations are social, some in the business world, and some romantic, the reactions of the "answering" planets can easily be translated to another sphere, and remain both typical and indicative of their interaction with the central planet. Venus and Mercury are given two roles each to reflect their "positive" and their "negative" sides.

1. Central Planet: The Sun

The sun has just been promoted to a position of greater authority. He talks with each of the people in his department who will be working for him—some of whom have been passed over. The sun is elated, but a little nervous. The sun asks: "How do you think it will be working together?"

Another sun: "This may come as a surprise to you, but I turned down the job. So long—I've got bigger things in mind."

Moon: "I know it will be difficult for you at first, but I will do all I can to help. Just remember, I have good days and bad days."

Mercury #1: "I'm all for it; you deserve the job. I could handle it, but I've got too many outside interests."

Mercury #2: "I hope you'll let me set up a new file system. Can I start right now?"

Venus #1: "You can handle change much better than I can, so I wish you well—but I do envy you the money."

Venus #2: "As you know, I rarely have trouble getting along with people, so I have no problem. Do you think we can get a new paint job?"

Mars: "It really doesn't matter to me; I do my own thing anyway and intend to keep on doing it. Any objections?"

Jupiter: "I know you'll probably get bogged down the way you always do, so I'll help out by giving you some of my ideas. Want to hear some?"

Saturn: "I guess my time hasn't come yet, but I really don't envy you. You've got a tough row to hoe."

Uranus: "Oh, hadn't you heard? I'm transferring to new-product development. You'll miss me? Can't imagine why."

Neptune: "I've got mixed emotions, and I'd like to talk to you privately. How about a drink after work?"

Pluto: "I think it best I don't say anything."

Best bet for the sun: Mars.

Worst bet for the sun: Pluto.

2. Central Planet: The Moon

The moon recently ran an ad in the local newspaper which read: "Shy, lonely single looking for pleasing partner. Must be sensitive, intelligent, and thoughtful. Object: Marriage, home, and children." These are some of the answers she received:

Sun: "I don't usually answer ads, and I'm very popular. But I think it's time I settled down. Call me sometime."

Another moon: "I've been looking all my life for someone who understands me; if I don't hear from you in two days, I'll know you don't care."

Mercury #1: "I'll be sociable for the two of us; but I don't know about the children bit. They can tie you down."

Mercury #2: "You sound like the quiet type, which is fine with me, but I hope you like a clean house and nutritional food."

Venus #1: "I am a stable, home-loving person, and it sounds as if we would be good together—if sex is as important to you as it is to me."

Venus #2: "I can't tell from your ad what your tastes are; I know I can be a 'pleasing partner'—as long as the surroundings are right."

Mars: "I don't know if I would describe myself as sensitive, but I've got to meet you anyway. How soon can we make a date?"

Jupiter: "Nothing ventured, nothing gained. I'll take a chance on love with you, if you'll give me lots of space."

Saturn: "I have lots of money and it sounds as if you've got everything else I want. What does your father do?"

Uranus: "To be honest, the whole thing sounds dull. Do you have any friends?"

Neptune: "I think I know what you're looking for, and I can help you find it."

Pluto: "If you are really all you say, I'm desperately in love; just don't break your promise."
  Best bet for the moon: Venus #1.
  Worst bet for the moon: Mars.

3. Central Planet: Mercury #1

Light-hearted, sociable Mercury is giving a party, to which are invited a variety of friends and acquaintances. As Mercury circulates the room, Mercury asks: "What's the most interesting book you've read lately/movie you've seen/thing you've heard?"

Sun: "I haven't been reading much. I've been too busy writing my autobiography. Want to read the manuscript?"

Moon: "I'm fascinated by *Remembrance of Things Past*, but it makes me want to cry. Got a Kleenex?"

Another Mercury #1: "I've got so much to talk about we could go on all night. Any possibility of your getting out of here?"

Mercury #2: "I can tell you what's wrong with any current book or movie you can name. Want to name one? I should have been a critic, you know."

Venus #1: "I don't go out much, and what I really enjoy is listening to music and eating chocolate."

Venus #2: "This is a great party. Who does your catering?"

Mars: "Did you hear they gave the Most Valuable Player award to the wimp, Joey D.? It makes my blood boil."

Jupiter: "Have you heard the one about the priest and the procurer? It's a real knee-slapper."

Saturn: "I'm just catching up with Burton's *Anatomy of Melancholy*. It has so much to say about the current human situation, and the way I feel most of the time."

Uranus: "There's an experiment going on in the southeastern quadrant of New Zealand which will eventually prove that sheep have more need for each other than people do."

Neptune: "Where are the snows of yesteryear, where have they gone?"

Pluto: "I can't talk about it in this crowd."
  Best bet for Mercury #1: Venus #2.
  Worst bet for Mercury #1: The moon.

4. Central Planet: Mercury #2

This planet is a worrier, so Mercury #2 has decided to find out *exactly* what each of the neighbors thinks about the way he or she maintains his or her property:

Sun: "Except for the way you yell at the children, you're a model neighbor. Did you know I'm running for mayor?"

Moon: "Your place is spotless, but I don't think you're happy. Let's talk."

Mercury #1: "Glad you called, I'm putting together a little party . . . Your property? Relax."

Another Mercury #2: "Why are you asking? Am I doing something wrong?"

Venus #1: "Wish I could keep a place so neat. Love your garden . . . how are your tomatoes doing?"

Venus #2: "I haven't any complaints."

Mars: "You're a crab, and the whole neighborhood knows it."

Jupiter: "Live and let live, I always say. I'm going to add on to my place. What to hear my plans?"

Saturn: "It's very comforting to have a solid citizen like you for a neighbor. What do you hear about me?"

Uranus: "How did you know I was thinking of starting a neighborhood association?"

Neptune: "No man is an island. The fence? Can't say I've really noticed."

Pluto: "I feel it's something we should discuss on a one-to-one basis. When can we meet?"
   Best bet for Mercury #2: The moon.
   Worst bet for Mercury #2: Jupiter.

5. Central Planet: Venus #1

This attractive planet has no lack of admirers. Lately Venus #1 has had a series of blind dates, and has asked each to wind up the evening at his or her place. Here are the responses each gave to Venus #1's provocative invitation.

Sun: "Delighted. I could tell you wanted more of my company."

Moon: "Let me think about what kind of mood I'm in."

Mercury #1: "Sorry, I've got a late date. Next time?"

Mercury #2: "Only if you've got some aspirins. I've got a headache."

Another Venus #1: "Love to; I haven't had dessert."

Venus #2: "If I say no, will you get mad?"

Mars: "I thought you'd never ask."

Jupiter: "It's been nice, but I've got to run. I feel a touch of claustrophobia coming on."

Saturn: "It's late and I've got to get up early; but I feel so comfortable with you I'll come."

Uranus: "Why don't we go for a midnight bike ride instead?"

Neptune: "I have the feeling we could talk all night."

Pluto: "I've been feeling the magnetism all evening. I may never go home."

Best bet for Venus #1: Saturn.
Worst bet for Venus #1: Venus #2.

6. Central Planet: Venus #2

Genial, noncontroversial Venus #2 has reluctantly taken on the task of getting out the vote for a local candidate. In this case, it is Venus #2's *responses* that indicate the potential relationship with each of the answering planets.

Sun: "They should be supporting a person with leadership qualities, like me."
"Of course."

Moon: "My gut feelings tell me he doesn't have his heart in the right place."
"*Who* told you?"

Mercury #1: "I heard him speak the other night; I like his style."
"Yes, he does make a good appearance."

Mercury #2: "I've heard some things about him I don't like."
  "Nobody's perfect."

Venus #1: "Nobody's going to tell *me* who to vote for."
  "I'm only suggesting."

Another Venus #2: "What do you think?"
  "I don't know—what do you think?"

Mars: "I want to see some action in this town. Is he a fighter?"
  "I hope not; I hate violence."

Jupiter: "Frankly, he sounds like a jerk. What are you doing working for him?"
  "Only my civic duty."

Saturn: "Where does he stand on taxes?"
  "What an intelligent question!"

Uranus: "I'm organizing for the opposition candidate; your man is too conservative."
  "Perhaps his suits are a bit dull."

Neptune: "I don't pay much attention to politics."
  "Sorry to have bothered you."

Pluto: "I don't sense conviction in your voice."
  "Do you want me to talk louder?"
  Best bet for Venus #2: The sun.
  Worst bet for Venus #2: Neptune.

7. Central Planet: Mars

Mars is dying to try hang-gliding and has decided to do it on the spur of the moment. In looking for a companion, Mars gets these responses from various friends.

Sun: "Piece of cake, but I can't make it today."

Moon: "You'll never get me up in one of those things . . . but what a great sensation it must be."

Mercury #1: "Rather not do it myself, but can I come along and take pictures?"

Mercury #2: "Are you sure all that fresh air is really good for you?"

Venus #1: "Sounds exhausting; why don't you come over to dinner afterward?"

Venus #2: "What shall I wear?"

Another Mars: "Anything you can do I can do better. When do we leave?"

Jupiter: "Sensational idea. Maybe we can teach each other a few things."

Saturn: "I'd rather not, but what can you tell me about the investment possibilities connected with the sport?"

Uranus: "Sure I'll go, but it's old hat. Have you tried it with just one wing?"

Neptune: "I may be able to get it together by this afternoon. I'll call you back this time, I promise."

Pluto: "Let's have a contest."
  Best bet for Mars: Jupiter.
  Worst bet for Mars: Saturn.

8. Central Planet: Jupiter

Jupiter has just come back from an extended trip abroad and is trying to put together a group of people to see his or her slides; Jupiter's offering a potluck supper and a prize to the person who can correctly identify all of the subjects. Here's what Jupiter gets back from the people invited:

Sun: "The last time you were the only one who got to say anything."

Moon: "I hope this doesn't hurt your feelings, but slide shows make me nervous."

Mercury #1: "Can I bring some of my slides, too? There's plenty I haven't shown you."

Mercury #2: "Give me a little time to think about it."

Venus #1: "I was planning to spend a quiet evening at home, but I'll come if we can spend a little time by ourselves later."

Venus #2: "Who else will be there?"

Mars: "Hell, no. I'd rather see things in person."

Another Jupiter: "Are you going to drone on like the last time? I'll bring a bottle."

Saturn: "How much is the prize?"

Uranus: "I've just discovered a great new lens. Can I see if it works on your projector?"

Neptune: "I would love to experience the beauty you have seen. I'll try not to be late."

Pluto: "I think you've got something up your sleeve. What's the catch?"
    Best bet for Jupiter: Mercury #1.
    Worst bet for Jupiter: Pluto.

9. Central Planet: Saturn

Saturn has been hospitalized with a bad case of exhaustion from overwork. While patient with his present condition, he is terribly concerned about how things are going back at the office, where he is president and chief financial officer. He asks each of his visitors from the office the same question: "Should I be worried about anything?"

Sun: "Relax; I've taken over and everything is going splendidly. In fact, morale seems even better than before."

Moon: "Now don't you worry about a thing; you'll just make yourself sicker, and I couldn't stand how that would make me feel."

Mercury #1: "We're all having a ball. Want to hear the latest gossip?"

Mercury #2: "I'm worrying for the two of us. What was our first symptom? You see, I've got this funny pain . . ."

Venus #1: "I can't imagine why, but people keep coming to me with their troubles. You wouldn't believe the work!"

Venus #2: "You look wonderful! By the way, I certainly hope your little problem won't delay our bonuses."

Mars: "What a relief not having you around, you drag! Ha, ha . . . only kidding."

Jupiter: "Now I'm taking the liberty of putting that little plan of mine in action. What's the matter? . . . Nurse! Nurse!"

Another Saturn: "Can't bear to think what first-quarter profits will look like. Is this a well-run hospital?"

Uranus: "Let's approach this thing logically. First, let's look at the accounts we don't have to worry about, then . . ."

Neptune: "Let's step back and look at the larger picture. In today's socioeconomic climate . . ."

Pluto: "Don't listen to what anyone else tells you. I'm the one who has the situation under control."

    Best bet for Saturn: Uranus.
    Worst bet for Saturn: Mercury #1.

10. Central Planet: Uranus

This rather impersonal planet sometimes plunges in where others fear to tread. He is conducting a telephone survey on the sex habits of the community in which he lives; he will later publish it through the university where he teaches sociology. In attempting to prove that virtually no one is wedded to traditional attitudes these days, he asks two questions: "Do you consider yourself a good sex partner?" and "What is the most innovative thing you do in bed?"

Sun: "I am pretty good, if I have to say so myself. Are you going to use my name?"

Moon: "It's much too emotional a subject for me to discuss over the phone; doesn't it make *you* uncomfortable?"

Mercury #1: "What a good idea—wish I'd thought of it. Can I write up your results for the local paper?"

Mercury #2: "I pride myself on doing everything perfectly. As for the second question, didn't you ever hear that Virgo is the most experimental sign in the zodiac?"

Venus #1: "I never thought about it much. I just do it and love it . . . *everything*."

Venus #2: "I really don't know what you're talking about."

Mars: "Did you ever hear of a sexual athlete? Let me tell you how I . . ."

Jupiter: "Anything goes among friends."

Saturn: "I try to keep up with all the latest techniques, but there's so much to read I get confused when I try to do it."

Another Uranus: "Just a minute, I'll go get my notes."

Neptune: "Did you ever try doing it to Debussy's 'La Mer'? What a high!"

Pluto: "If I told you you wouldn't believe it—so I'll keep it to myself."

Best bet for Uranus: Mercury #2.

Worst bet for Uranus: The moon.

11. Central Planet: Neptune

This mystical planet loves to get out of this world, and will take every opportunity to. Neptune has discovered a new medium and wants to have a seance. Here's how Neptune's friends react:

Sun: "Sorry; I've got a PTA meeting. Call me next time you want to play cards."

Moon: "I've heard wonderful things about her; I'll bring the candles and incense."

Mercury #1: "Whom are we going to try to contact?"

90

Mercury #2: "You know, it's not healthy for all those people to sit around in an airless room holding hands."

Venus #1: "You really believe in that stuff, huh?"

Venus #2: "Seances are terribly romantic; I'll come."

Mars: "You're kidding."

Jupiter: "How fascinating! I share your interest in the metaphysical, but I hope it doesn't take too long."

Saturn: "Life is difficult enough in this world. Think I'll pass it up."

Uranus: "Good. This will give me an opportunity to test the theory of electrobiomagnetic intergalactic energy."

Another Neptune: "There are more things in this world than most people dream of. I'll bring some hash."

Pluto: "I'll join the circle, but I can't be responsible for anything that happens."
Best bet for Neptune: Venus #2.
Worst bet for Neptune: The sun.

12. Central Planet: Pluto

This passionate planet has had a serious affair with a number of people in the office, but is never satisfied. Here's how the rest react to Pluto's subtle but seductive approach, which begins, "Do you sense the magnetism between us?"

Sun: "It's good to know you find me attractive, but I'm attached."

Moon: "I'm sure a lot of people don't understand you, but I do."

Mercury #1: "I just thought it was warm in here."

Mercury #2: "You have an annoying habit of putting your hands on people. Please don't touch me."

Venus #1: "Is that what it is? I call it something else. See you after work."

Venus #2: "What a lovely voice you have. Please pass the sugar."

Mars: "Buzz off before I show you how my magnetism works."

Jupiter: "I don't think we have a thing in common, but let's give it a whirl anyway."

Saturn: "But what about my family ... my job ... my future?"

Uranus: "Sorry, I don't get involved, but what do you call that theory?"

Neptune: "Yes, it's absolutely spiritual, but I don't want to get hurt."

Another Pluto: "We'd end up destroying each other; anyway, I've got something else going. Well, OK."

Best bet for Pluto: Pluto.

Worst bet for Pluto: Mercury #2.

CAPRICORN DAY-BY-DAY
PREDICTIONS, 1984

January 1984

Astronote to Capricorn: This year it's your turn to reap the marvelous benefits of the planet Jupiter in your own sign. Jupiter moves into Capricorn this month and stays there the entire year, bringing lots of goodies along the way. Jupiter's benevolence can be very discreet, however, and that means you can't just sit back and wait for the pennies to fall from heaven. Jupiter works best when you work in tandem with him, looking around every corner for the opportunity that may be standing there. If you are shortsighted you could shortchange yourself.

Another influence you will have to keep alert for is that of the planet Neptune which moves into your sign this year for a rather long stay. Neptune's influence is rather diffuse, but it can be felt and used in a number of ways. One thing Neptune may bring this year—particularly to those born in late December—is a kind of confusion about what your ultimate goals and ambitions are. Neptune tends to throw a haze over the future and sometimes you have to be ruthless in stripping it away. One of Neptune's theme songs is "I'm always chasing rainbows." On the other hand Neptune in Capricorn can bring the benefits of new inspiration to members of that sign. It may start as a kind of divine dissatisfaction, but Neptune's ultimate influence can be to bring out creative thinking or latent talents you have refused or chosen not to recognize. This is particularly so in the case of Capricorn who doesn't have time for much besides the purely practical.

All in all, it looks like one of the most potentially fruitful years that the sign of Capricorn has enjoyed for a number of years. Put your best face forward and greet 1984 with a great big smile.

Sunday, January 1: You start off the year on a thoughtful note; it's a day of "internal review" and planning for the future. Some recent sour notes in your life have sweetened a bit and you feel you can see light at the end of the tunnel. Some secrets that surface are helpful to your plans.

Monday, January 2: MOON IN CAPRICORN. As the moon starts its monthly swing through your sign you get a surge of energy and a feeling of power. It's not just a feeling, because you've got a good chance of getting whatever you go after today. You have the look of authority and you find you can act the part. One of your relationships may feel the brunt of your extra edge today.

Tuesday, January 3: Stick to your guns and do not waver; there's no reason for you to kowtow to anyone today. You prove your worth by finishing off a big job and by doing it well. With your sense of timing as good as it is now, you should strike while the iron is hot to get some things you feel are coming to you.

Wednesday, January 4: A challenge presents itself today but you are more than up to it. Now the crowd will be following you! Where you lead them is into the ground floor of a new deal that is shaping up to be rather great. Don't let anyone forget that you pioneered this enterprise.

Thursday, January 5: You can watch your pennies without being labeled "tightwad"; future security is the thing to think of now. And be aware that you don't have endless resources of energy either and have to save in that area too. Wait a bit and see which way the wind blows: you may be too emotional about the subject at the moment to be very effective anyway.

Friday, January 6: With your eye for quality, you know a good deal when you see it. Today when something pleases your eye, be sure to grab it, and you'll have a prize in your pocket. Someone of the opposite sex looks pretty good to you today, too—especially when he or she helps you out of a tight spot. The day's lucky number is 3.

Saturday, January 7: Today is one of those days when if you want it done you'd better do it yourself; don't rely on anyone else, no matter how willing they are to do some running for you. Keep a sharp lookout when something strikes you as a little fuzzy—it probably is. Get the facts and all the facts.

Sunday, January 8: You may feel like dancing around the facts today. Someone is trying to pin you down more than you like. Another someone deserves a really nice "hi" from you; be your sweet charming self when you call or write. You can be very creative when you want to. The number 5 may be important.

Monday, January 9: It's possible to splurge on some luxuries without totally getting in over your head. You feel so relieved today you could get a little carried away with an entertaining scheme; keep it within bounds. The occasion could be a reunion with a relative who hasn't been in the picture recently—be on your best behavior!

Tuesday, January 10: Some reminiscing that was done yesterday gave you a sense of roots and focused your attention on your own home ground. Home and family are extraordinarly important to you, so you should be particularly careful in signing agreements and finalizing terms in anything that pertains to that area.

Wednesday, January 11: This is a really productive day for you. Some recent developments have put a bigger load on your shoulders, but you are not only up to it—you are ahead of it. You should feel proud of yourself for the accomplishment—as well as for the nice things you are doing for an older person who needs TLC.

Thursday, January 12: It's too soon to act, but you don't have to sit idly by; assess the total picture so you will be ready to move when the time is right. You are right to feel that you've got the power in this situation, and your own sense of what's right will make you use it properly.

97

Friday, January 13: Pleasure may be at the top of your list of priorities today—you're in the mood not only for romance, but a romantic dinner as well. Relax and enjoy—though you may have to take time out to set somebody straight about what he or she owes you in the way of information. The number to watch is 1.

Saturday, January 14: Slow the pace just enough to get a better view of the passing scene and to set your house in order, so to speak. The more you create order around you the more comfortable and secure you will feel. You might even have fun working in tandem with someone who knows how to make play out of work.

Sunday, January 15: Sit back and leave the driving to someone else today; a low-key approach will give you the rest and respite you need. You may feel that a good workout on the tennis court or sports field would rev you up; good possibility—but don't overdo.

Mid-month memo to Capricorn: Even though January is your birthday month it can feel endless and get quite boring. If you are afflicted with the mid-winter blues, here are some typical Capricorn activities or interests that might gave your spirits a lift.

Take a carpentry or woodworking course; see a chiropractor; get a new haircut; take a math course; go rock-climbing; do volunteer work in a home for the aged; get into local politics; take up pottery; dabble in real estate; go to a dude ranch; turn the basement into a rec room; study architecture; become a volunteer crime preventor; start an old coin collection; go spelunking.

Monday, January 16: Your mind is very much on your work today; in fact, there may be some kind of confrontation with your boss. It's possible you are evaluating just how important this job is to you. Do you need this aggravation? A couple of office buddies try to help you laugh it off. The lucky number is 4.

Tuesday, January 17: You've decided you are really going to keep your eyes open for some new opportunities; in fact you will go further and actually look into contacts someone gives you. It's important to be as discreet as possible. Meanwhile, cool the game-playing with a romantic partner; you don't have time for it.

Wednesday, January 18: You may have to face a kind of showdown with your one-and-only today. You are really going to have to dance around the central issue; be as tactful as possible and don't push your luck. In fact, why not get something really nice in the way of a gift to help smooth things over.

Thursday, January 19: You are in a particularly charitable mood today and may decide that some extracurricular work in one of the service fields would do you a lot of good. This spirtual sense comes to you through a strange coincidence you have a feeling is really not a coincidence at all. Today's number is 7.

Friday, January 20: What a day to make a power play! You've got some mighty solid backing in the form of influential people who like your slightly conservative style. Go for what you want with confidence and you just may get it. Someone of the opposite sex finds your way of doing things very interesting.

Saturday, January 21: You may be able to feel like a relatively fat cat today with your recent gains. Your optimistic mood is helpful in getting all your ducks in a row for a long-range plan you've got in mind. You are able to think beyond the purely mundane details and envision a beautiful future.

Sunday, January 22: It's clear you've made a breakthrough; just look at how many people are playing back your message. Obviously you've gotten the point across and shoved an old stumbling block out of the way. Good for you.

Monday, January 23: You are so dead-sure you are right that you are willing to put your reputation on the line. There's no doubt in your mind that you understand the practical aspects of the situation better than anyone else. You've got some pretty strong opposition but you are up to it. A friend says "thanks" for an old favor.

Tuesday, January 24: Dole out both your time and your energy with a lot of care today; you've got a lot to do and if you scatter your forces you may get rattled. Some swift changes may be a bit disconcerting, but in the course of them you see your position as pretty solid.

Wednesday, January 25: You are the original when it comes to building your way to fame and fortune from a firm ground of facts and figures. Put that ability to work today when you must renegotiate with someone. The facts will make your far-off dream a closer possibility. Later on relax with some old friends who feel like celebrating.

Thursday, January 26: You see! It pays off to pick up the phone and ask for the answers you want. Your decisive action opens up some interesting avenues for your ideas. Don't get so caught up in business today that you slight someone close to you; he or she deserves some time and should be consulted about how to spend it.

Friday, January 27: There's sweet harmony at home and a lot of it is due to your efforts. You may literally be making music too as you discover a hidden talent—or at least an interest in that area. Don't play it down; you never know what can happen.

Saturday, January 28: You may feel like chucking it all today. It's not a bad idea to put off a few things you intended to do. You are better off waiting it out alone where your lack of patience will not be noticed. After all, it's your problem and you need time to work it out. The number 7 could be a winner.

Sunday, January 29: Waiting it out doesn't mean doing nothing at all. Stop brooding and get some background work going; you are in a good position to maneuver the situation. You get a lift when someone comes along with a little something that proves you are still loved and adored.

Monday, January 30: MOON IN CAPRICORN. There's nothing stopping you today; you've got both the will and the way. Your mind is going like sixty with new ideas and coming up with great answers about how to get them in the works. It's fine to be independent and energetic, but just don't overdo.

Tuesday, January 31: Among the positive things you can count on today is your own good judgment about a member of the opposite sex. Your sense of adventure and desire for independence are both on high, and you are able to go way beyond your usual boundaries today and make out quite well. Some new people are with you as you ride the crest.

February 1984

Astronote to Capricorn: With Valentine's Day just around the corner it's the likely moment to look at Capricorn in love. Those who have been involved with members of this sign might say that "Capricorn in love" is a contradiction in terms. However, this sentiment is most likely to be expressed by those who have loved but lost someone born under this difficult sign. Perhaps they have made the fatal mistake: making it obvious to Capricorn that they were in pursuit.

The typical Capricornian love affair scenario starts off so quietly you might not even notice. One could easily mistake Capricorn's romantic interest as a desire for friendship and nothing more. Both sexes born under this sign are so discreet and closed-in that it is difficult to pick up even a clue that he or she has anything else in mind. The famous Capricorn remoteness is an unfortunate characteristic—at least when it comes to attracting and encouraging love partners. The

Capricorn usually seems so unapproachable that only the pushiest will dare to approach; what often happens then is that Capricorn takes off like a scared mountain goat. The result is a fact of astrological life: Capricorn is a late-bloomer in terms of love and marriage.

Capricorn is a patient sign, and it takes a lot of patience on the part of his or her would-be romantic partner to cultivate the relationship. It not only starts out slowly; it can also take eons to develop into what could even remotely be called a passionate pairing. Those who can pass the test—and Saturn-ruled Capricorn tends to make people prove themselves—will end up in a stable, predictable relationship with a loyal and supportive partner. Who could ask for anything more? A lot of people—which is why Capricorn is not regarded as the most marriageable of the signs.

Wednesday, February 1: You don't mind feeling a bit like you are overworked because the rewards are substantial. By digging in and showing your stuff you are putting money in the bank for the future as well. You look very good against the competition and it should make you feel a bit smug.

Thursday, February 2: It occurs to you that the reason you can't make up your mind is that there are too many options; be drastic in cutting them down, because a decision is the most important thing here. You may find yourself working in tandem toward a new goal with some very enterprising people. Take a clue from their style. The number 9 may be important.

Friday, February 3: Your quick snap-to yesterday proved you can do more than one thing well; it may net you a short but interesting business trip. The indication of approval makes you feel very good about yourself. You even find that others are now following your lead.

Saturday, February 4: There's a nice spirit of give-and-take on the home scene now; your opposite member reaches out to make a conciliatory gesture, and you should respond in kind. Some young people may need a little consideration too—don't be too harsh with ground rules. It's best to give a little to get what you want.

Sunday, February 5: You are going to have to get into it today as much as you would like to avoid a pitched battle that starts among siblings. Speak with authority, but retain your sense of humor. Some really creative ideas have been buzzing around in your head lately. Be sure to get them down on paper.

Monday, February 6: There is nothing that makes you feel happier than a sense of your own place, and you are enjoying familiar ground now in particular. The sense of security it gives you should help both to overcome some obstacles and to get a difficult person over to your side. The day's number is 4.

Tuesday, February 7: Someone near to you needs a lot of reassurance now; even if you don't feel 100 percent up yourself, try to appear strong and solid. Those ideas you've been jotting down should get a careful analysis so you can put them in order for submission.

Wednesday, February 8: These days you seem to get more satisfaction from your home than anything else. A redecorating project is not only fun, it helps pull you closer to a family member who wants to get involved. It's a good feeling to work in tandem. The number to watch is 6.

Thursday, February 9: Don't play games with a romantic partner now; it's important to see him or her in a realistic light. Remember, you get back what you give out, and you must admit your recent behavior has not been up to par. He or she is a little more complicated than you, and you should respect the difference.

Friday, February 10: You get a great kick out of life today, maybe because you do some of the things you like to do best. It starts your creative juices going and you see some real potential in something that's been just a hobby up to now. You could get some backing and make it work for profit.

Saturday, February 11: There's a focus on responsibilities today, and it may not be as stimulating as yesterday's activities. Some deadlines are pressing and you are going to have to put your nose to the grindstone if you are going to make them. Throw yourself into it and get the whole thing out of the way.

Sunday, February 12: You need to relax today; some worry about your current situation is really pointless since you can't do anything about it today. Let another, more playful type, possibly a Leo, get your mind on something more amusing. The number 1 is lucky today.

Monday, February 13: You may run smack into an abrasive encounter today, and it could throw you. Make your comeback by taking a deep breath and willing yourself some new psychic energy. Don't be extravagant with anything today, including your emotions. Toss out some unneeded and hindering materials.

Tuesday, February 14: The past few days' mood of gloom and doom vanishes totally and you feel a lot better—especially when an exciting invitation comes your way. Accept, but make sure you do the necessaries as well. You are a good negotiator today, so take the opportunity to wind up some legal matters.

Wednesday, February 15: It's always tricky to handle somebody else's money, and you may find yourself doing just that today. Don't turn any part of it over to others. If you do a careful job and make a good showing, it could mean money in your pocket as well. Be sure to read all the fine print.

Mid-month memo to Capricorn: If you are a Capricorn and you read your "love profile" at the beginning of this month, you may be a bit depressed; Capricorns often are. However, be assured that there *are* compatible people in the zodiac who would consider one of life's greatest achievements trapping a Capricorn. And, quite logically, the sign's best bets for lasting love are the other very achievement-oriented signs.

Number one on the list is another Capricorn. This is one of those cases where like truly attracts like. A rather close second is Scorpio, who—like Capricorn—must live well to love well. There is a determination to both signs that makes them able to tough it out if rough spots occur in the relationship; because common material goals are so important. Taurus is not bad with Capricorn because as earth signs both have the same practical frame of reference. Taurus, however, may be a little too laid-back for hard-driving Capricorn. This match-up works best when the female is the Taurean. Cancer is Capricorn's polar opposite and they often do attract. Cancer's intense desire for both material and emotional security is generally satisfied by Capricorn. The remaining water sign, Pisces, is a disaster with "together" Capricorn, and the third earth sign, Virgo, may want Capricorn, but the reverse is rarely the case.

Surprisingly, it is the air sign Aquarius who can often find bliss sharing a life with Capricorn. Neither is too comfortable with extreme closeness and both tend to apply logic to problems. It may be a marriage of convenience, but both sides usually benefit. Of the fire signs, Leo stands a chance with Capricorn because both like to be "in the money"; Leo, however, may have his or her warm heart bruised a bit by Capricorn's natural reserve which Leo can mistake for coldness.

Thursday, February 16: Whatever your bailiwick, it should get a lot more exciting today. Anything can happen from meeting a potential marriage partner to having a great job opportunity drop in your lap. You won't see any of it if you aren't alert and willing to be a bit flexible. Seize the day!

Friday, February 17: If at all possible, take some time out today to let your mind soar far ahead of your body. A little thoughtfulness will give you a real sense of well-being. Don't fear that you are being idle; a lot of things are brewing in your subconscious that will serve you very well later on. The lucky number is 6.

Saturday, February 18: What was under the surace bobs up today and startles you; you had no idea you had feelings and attitudes like this. They didn't come from nowhere, so take the time to try to integrate them into your present experience. It may be a bit spooky when an old friend, too, seems to come out of nowhere.

Sunday, February 19: You find yourself coming out into the world today and leaving your pensive state behind. The first thing you see is a fabulous opportunity to grab something important—possibly in the way of a new job. You could use your extra power today to improve a domestic situation as well; make the change you want now.

Monday, February 20: It's a bit of a surprise to see how many people seem to want your advice and counsel now; be generous, but don't let anyone take advantage of you. You do feel very outgoing today, however, so it might be the ideal time to offer your services to a group that could use them.

Tuesday, February 21: You really feel like going it alone now, but your wisest course is to enlist the cooperation of others. It's possible to be too independent sometimes. Curb your tendency to want to break away and run ahead. Time is on your side and there is really not such a hurry.

Wednesday, February 22: If you are honest with yourself, you'll feel like being honest with others today. When you reach out you get a wonderful playback of similar emotions and affection. Someone older—possibly a female—is your inspiration in trying to achieve this new and better emotional climate.

Thursday, February 23: You could be all over the lot if you accepted all the invitations that have been coming your way. You are particularly intrigued by the chance

to meet people whose brains you can pick about travel—
even if in reality it is far off for you. A Sagittarian may
be just the ticket to satisfy your curiosity.

Friday, February 24: Nobody is going to catch you
sleeping at the switch today. Anyone who thinks you
haven't got your eye on every detail is in for a rude
shock. You are wise not to take anything for granted
today; check it all out. You may even turn up something that was lost. The number 4 could be important.

Saturday, February 25: You are going to have to be
very quick on the trigger today when someone fires a
question or suggestion at you. Prompt response will
prove your creativity and your ability to pick up on
nuances. Sometimes people get the idea that you are
not too subtle. Get the message across that you can be.

Sunday, February 26: MOON IN CAPRICORN. You
are in such a mellow mood that you don't even blink an
eye when a family member goes all out on a purchase.
Since it is for everyone to enjoy and admire, you don't
mind a bit. In fact, you are so home-oriented that this
kind of thing only makes you feel that much more
secure. You love togetherness.

Monday, February 27: It's obvious to some people who
count that you are willing to work with the organization
and identify your success with it. That puts you in a
great spot and gives you the opportunity to express
your ideas to receptive ears. You are off to a new start,
but need some private time to take it all in.

Tuesday, February 28: Buying and selling is very much
part of the scene today. Even if you do not actually
make a transaction, you will be consulted. Give it your
full attention because there could be an interesting deal
in the offing. Some economic sacrifices may be necessary
because of recent changes in your domestic arrangement.

Wednesday, February 29: It's very possible for you to
look at things in the cold hard light of reality today.

What you see may prompt you to end a relationship that really no longer works for either of you. You may polish off some other matters too to make way for your next move ahead.

March 1984

Astronote to Capricorn: As with every sign, there is more than one type of Capricorn. Among the many astrological factors that differentiate person from person under each sign is the actual *date* of birth. Each sign is divided into three ten-day segments or decanates. For Capricorn the first decanate includes people born from the beginning of the sign until about January 1 or 2. These are Capricorns who come under the direct and sole rulership of the planet Saturn and consequently exhibit both Capricornian and Saturnine characteristics most strongly. Here are the bigger strivers, and often the greater achievers. They may also be the most difficult to move, however, and be prone to despondency and depression.

Second-decanate Capricorns, born from about January 1 or 2 to about January 11 or 12, have the planet Venus as a co-ruler with Saturn. This is a decidedly softening influence, and there is inclined to be more warmth in this type of Capricorn. He or she may be more of a plodder rather than an upward climber, however. Venus can be a little lazy. Second-decanate Capricorns are the more domesticated type of the nimble mountain goat that is the sign's symbol. Third-decanate Capricorns are born from around January 11 and 12 to the end of the sign. Speaking of nimble, these are the most mentally agile Capricorns, with quick and precise minds bestowed on them by the corulership of the planet Mercury. It is among this group that one tends to find the Capricorn who marries science to business and makes his or her mark. In terms of the emotional life, however, these more "mental" Capricorns may apply logic as well as practicality to the subject of relationships and analyze them to death.

Thursday, March 1: Indecision can be particularly painful to Capricorn. In order to end your current bout with it you will have to do some self-analysis and figure out what your real wants are, and how they balance out against the desires of others. This internal argument may be sidetracked by an interesting deal someone brings to your attention—possibly to do with publishing.

Friday, March 2: You are more than ready for a break in routine; you are just in the mood to exercise your individuality and try out some new ways of expressing yourself. The chance to do so may be connected with a trip—possibly not a long one. A contact you make today is key to the day's excitement—and the future as well.

Saturday, March 3: You may insist that everyone in the household get organized along with you today. Lots of lists and stock-taking are on the agenda, and all with the practical purpose of getting the budget in order. Everyone is pretty cooperative, and even siblings seem to get a lot out of working together.

Sunday, March 4: Yesterday's round of activity has left you feeling pretty satisfied with your and yours. Your excellent mood lets your sense of humor come smiling through, and a good time is had by all. One reason for your good feelings is that you've gotten a load off your mind. The number 3 should be a winner.

Monday, March 5: Devotion to home and hearth earns you a lot of appreciation today. Your personal involvement in the things that make life nicer to live there is not only noticed but tangibly rewarded. You feel and know you are loved. An interesting individual—possibly an Aquarian—crosses your path and influences things today.

Tuesday, March 6: Today looks like a blue plate special with a little bit of a lot of good things. Pleasure is emphasized, as is communication between loved ones. Put those together and you have a rather exciting scenario. Whatever happens, it's a day to ask for what you really want—and have the possibility of getting it.

Wednesday, March 7: Someone new is introduced into the plot today, and may cause a flurry of activity, even signal a celebration. You are very much a part of it, and your own home ground may even be the stage. Good thing you have been particularly concerned with making a beautiful one. The lucky number is 6.

Thursday, March 8: If you've got a sneaking suspicion that something is not quite right, you are wise to act on it. Some small but significant matters may have been overlooked. Better to fix them now and risk causing someone some embarrassment than have things bollixed up later on.

Friday, March 9: You operate the way most employers like—you spend more time on action than on words. That tendency pays off handsomely now, but you get a big challenge along with the reward. There's no doubt that you can keep up your steady-as-she-goes efforts, so don't worry.

Saturday, March 10: You prove today that you are able to do "visionary" work as well as the usual daily grind. Some long-range ideas you project get the attention and the admiration of a few people. One particularly farsighted type likes your style so much you decide to dó something together.

Sunday, March 11: It's a good day for you to flex your determination muscles. When you show the kind of strength you are capable of you ensure your solid position vis-à-vis leases and property rights in their legal aspects. You do have time for romance, however, and it may involve a rather fiery individual.

Monday, March 12: Everyone you have to deal with today proves to be in a highly cooperative mood, and it makes matters go smoothly. You learn through a contact (possibly a Gemini) that there are some interesting deals available. You at least find out that what you own now is good and secure.

Tuesday, March 13: Someone you work with admires your special talents and seeks you out with the idea of cooperating on a project. Don't grab it immediately because you may find some shaky details in the overall scheme. First consider the alternatives and then decide whether to act on this one.

Wednesday, March 14: Rumors may be flying today and some of them sound pretty tempting. Your best course is to stick with the way you have been doing things for now. As you go along, you will get a more complete story, but you'll have to read between the lines to get it. Watch out for someone rather wily.

Thursday, March 15: You could sell just about anything today, including yourself. The magnetism you project draws people to you, so it doesn't take much effort to become a go-getter. What virtually falls in your lap comes from someone who believes in you now, but wasn't so sure before.

Mid-month memo to Capricorn: No matter which decanate a Capricorn is born in, he or she will almost inevitably be a person for whom convention is more comfortable than innovation. Capricorns tend to live by the rules, particularly those of society. Extreme behavior or eccentricity is not Capricorn's cup of tea—and he or she will not appreciate it in others. The mate or partner of a Capricorn must be prepared to tread the straight and narrow, and run the risk of criticism if he or she strays from the conventional path. The way to get a Capricorn to loosen up a bit is to create an occasion where it is the order of the day to do something out of the ordinary, for instance, a costume party. Capricorn will spare no expense or mental effort in coming up with the best costume. And under such conditions one will probably see the dry Capricorn sense of humor in action. It's generally a little acid but it's usually on the mark.

Friday, March 16: There's been a lot of running around in circles and what appears to be a gigantic misunderstanding caused by a lack of communication between the right parties. Today it all becomes clear as crystal, and all it takes is one little phone call. Too bad all the fuss couldn't have been avoided, but sometimes it's just not possible.

Saturday, March 17: It may have occurred to you that you are sometimes too hard on yourself. Do a little self-evaluating today; things you see as faults may be only in your own eyes. It's important to see yourself for what you really are—and what you can contribute. You may be pleasantly surprised!

Sunday, March 18: Your mind may again be on where you are going. Set your sights high in terms of business achievement, because there is nothing to hold you back now. Go forward as firmly and swiftly as you can, branching out and letting others notice your acumen and abilities.

Monday, March 19: As if on cue, someone lets you know today that you are looking good in terms of your achievements. It makes you feel even better when a couple of others come to you for consultation. Just be a little wary of too much flattery; someone could be trying to manipulate you. If you keep your goals firmly in mind it won't be possible.

Tuesday, March 20: Roll up your sleeves and dig in today; no one knows better than you that you don't get anything for nothing. Don't forget that appearances count for quite a lot, however. Sharpen your style of dressing as you plan a new start. Your peers give you some approval and it spurs you on. Today 9 is a strong number.

Wednesday, March 21: Sometimes the best is to step out of the way and let the crowd go by. Today that's a good course until you can really see which way the wind is blowing. You won't lose any time if you spend it doing your homework, gathering facts and figures.

Thursday, March 22: You feel like kicking it all over today in favor of fun and frolic. Go ahead! You can do the most for yourself and for others today by socializing with a lot of people. You bring joy where you go. Don't forget to bring a little of it to a friend who can't get around.

Friday, March 23: Some confidential information is finally revealed and it enables you to correct an error in interpretation. Best to get it down on paper and finish up this thing once and for all. You've got a clear path for progress now and you shouldn't let anything stand in the way. The lucky number is 4.

Saturday, March 24: MOON IN SCORPIO. Your slightly serious mood of yesterday vanishes like lightning and you feel it even in your tendency to dress up in something light and bright. Variety is the order of the day, and it could include a really good one-on-one with a member of the opposite sex.

Sunday, March 25: You are able to throw yourself into domestic obligations with a lot of feeling now that you understand the slightly indifferent attitude on the part of someone important. It just required a clear explanation—which makes sense to you. Your morale is lifted by the experience and you are able to adjust your own attitude.

Monday, March 26: Things are pretty good these days—good enough to make you reflect on how much you really have. As you assess personal possessions, you get a picture of your own real values. Things are important, but you refuse to be owned by them. There are too many other more vital issues, like relationships.

Tuesday, March 27: With your new view of things, you give a lot of intense energy to your home and parental involvements. You exercise good judgment when you figure out some ways to make a little go a little farther. Future security is as important as present factors. A good number is 8 today.

Wednesday, March 28: Your mind is much easier about the state of your personal economy; you've not only figured out how to save, you've actually got more coming in. It's a result of your willingness to take some steps you were indecisive about before. The sense of inner satisfaction is a good feeling.

Thursday, March 29: Today you are determined to get out and get around. Some new people you have met open new doors you can walk through and you express yourself in new ways. Part of the action today involves relatives—possibly siblings—and a fun visit could result.

Friday, March 30: This is a catch-up day and a time to collect yourself for weekend activity. You are feeling a little uneasy but can't put your finger on it; a friend or neighbor does. You realize you've temporarily lost your sense of perspective, and resolve to get it back. An emotional person figures big, and could be the cause of your uneasiness.

Saturday, March 31: You are in high spirits today, and it's good for everybody. No matter what happens, you take it with a delightful sense of humor. It seems to be catching, and you become very popular quickly. Don't miss an opportunity to express yourself on paper today— you'll be at your best.

April 1984

Astronote to Capricorn: One of the ways to understand a sign is to look at its position in the zodiac. There is a logical progression from young-as-springtime Aries to a world-weary Pisces, and the zodiac as a whole represents the total of human existence. Capricorn, as the tenth sign, stands guard over the tenth station of the zodiac—the sphere of power and achievement in the world of getting and spending. There is a natural urge in everyone to prove oneself on the battleground of competition for the material things of this world; by virtue of the sign's zodiacal heritage, that urge is usually at its peak in Capricorn.

Prestige, honor, and standing in the community go hand in hand with material wealth and, for Capricorn, are equally important to a sense of self-worth. It is unfortunate but true that the tainted word ambition must also be mentioned. One reason people sometimes back off from them is that they sense in Capricorns the desire for success at all costs, and it is not always such a pleasant fragrance. Although, of course, there are many exceptions, the Capricorns of this world are usually the ones so determined to get ahead that they will sacrifice even love on the altar of self-aggrandizement. Not true of all Capricorns? Yes, but scratch an unsuccessful Capricorn and you will generally find a rather bitter person. Power comes in many forms, however, and there are any number of arenas where one can amass prestige. That's why even at the humblest levels of human existence the best performer is often a Capricorn.

Sunday, April 1: You are generally not the world's greatest self-promoter, but today you mull over some bright, inventive ideas about how to sell yourself. Some of them grow out of a spirited conversation with other people who are definitely not run-of-the-mill. The discussion verges on an argument, but is really constructive for all involved.

Monday, April 2: Today you sharpen the pencil a little to bring home expenses more into line. Nobody gives you any objections, however, as your belt-tightening doesn't really hurt. It makes you feel a lot more secure, however, and you can tell that it rubs off on others when you get a nod of gratitude. The day's number is 2.

Tuesday, April 3: You can be pretty funny when you want to, and today you are urged to go into your act.

The playful spirit is upon you and you oblige, which is delightful to everyone. The group includes some pretty witty characters, so you make an even better showing when you top them.

Wednesday, April 4: Someone puts you to the test today, and it's up to you to prove you can come up to the mark. It may be a member of the opposite sex who throws down the gauntlet. You may decide, however, on a whole new set of ground rules between the two of you so that this kind of confrontation can be avoided in the future.

Thursday, April 5: New faces and new places are on the bill of fare today. You might find yourself actually going on a short trip—most likely for business. It's important that you clear up some unfinished things before you depart. A helpful person is willing to do some of the dirty work for you. The number to watch is 5.

Friday, April 6: It may be annoying when someone butts in and tries to tell you how to run things—at home or the office or even both. You know how important it is to keep the peace so you go out of your way to be nice even though you reject the advice. Your fairness is appreciated by others who observe it.

Saturday, April 7: You can't avoid the reality of what needs to be done—and your partner can't either. Grit your teeth and dig in, even though it is boring and routine. On top of it, you might have to spend extra time helping out someone who really needs you. Tomorrow is another day.

Sunday, April 8: Something that's been hanging over you gets settled and you win hands down. It makes you feel vindicated and ready to say "I told you so." Don't waste energy that way; pursue a fascinating person who appears and who could become more than a buddy.

Monday, April 9: You begin the week by ending something, and you see the road clear to move on. In taking a step forward you acquire some new problems, but they are the interesting kind. Start on the right foot by insisting on clear, concise explanations of some complicated matters. You'll get help from someone who knows the ropes. A lucky number for the day is 9.

Tuesday, April 10: You are numero uno today, and don't forget it. You can afford to be more daring in how you put yourself across to others. People have been giving you high marks recently for your self-starter reputation, and it could get you some important backing from a monied individual. Take a look over your shoulder, however, and watch out for a possibly dangerous Scorpio.

Wednesday, April 11: Pull in your horns a little today; it's time to do some soul-searching. You've been going at a pretty fast pace and you should take time out to renew yourself. In the process your psychic powers could bring you some startling and helpful revelations. Share some of your thoughts with a sensitive person who is willing to listen.

Thursday, April 12: Yesterday was like a shot in the arm to your intellectual vigor. You are determined to get a handle on some things that have long interested you; it may even mean back to school for you. The urge to travel is upon you and you may make some plans for it. The lucky number is 3.

Friday, April 13: A secret plan you have developed spurs you on to do the groundwork. You know it's something you've got to do solo. In terms of effort, you are willing to give it your all, because the goal that only you can see is worth it. Keep your intensity within bounds, however; nothing is worth killing yourself for and you tend to overdo.

Saturday, April 14: Good reports about you and your activities are played back to you today; it's great to have people working in your behalf. High prestige is attractive to a certain someone who offers to introduce you to someone important. Take him or her up on it, but be aware that there may be an ulterior motive.

Sunday, April 15: There's no doubt about the fact that your taste is excellent. Today someone appreciates it and makes a wonderful suggestion for adding to the beauty and luxury of your surroundings. You spend the day relaxing to the sweet strains of music that can soothe the savage beast.

Mid-month memo to Capricorn: Capricorn does not become successful without reason; his or her zodiacal heritage endows him or her not only with ambition, but the tools to implement it as well. For one thing, Capricorn is decisive. The expression "executive decision" may have been coined for Capricorn. Conclusions are not reached willy-nilly, however. There is a complete but speedy process whereby all the facts are taken into consideration before a decision is made. Yes, other signs can do that, but the point about Capricorn is that he or she does not extend the process, and is able to issue a decision at the critical moment. Another thing that characterizes Capricorn's decisiveness is foresight. What Capricorn decides is not only right for now, but usually serves some future goal or purpose as well. Cool, clearheaded, and generally collected, Capricorn is welcome in any circle where someone has got to decide.

Monday, April 16: You are not in the mood to be the hard-striving Capricorn today. It's OK once in a while to retire into your own private world and meditate on your many blessings. Others understand your temporary withdrawal from the world, and look at you with admiration for your ability to do so comfortably.

Tuesday, April 17: Today it's back to business, and you run smack into a problem. You realize it is necessary to take less now in order to get more later on; it's a minor sacrifice, however. A mate or partner doesn't see it that way; he or she just needs time to adjust. The number 8 is important today.

Wednesday, April 18: Life always has its compensations. Today you get a fabulous opportunity to extend your sphere of interest. It's good to know people at the top—and to think you may be there someday yourself. It's a nice piece of advertising for you as well. Some people have the grace to say "nice going."

Thursday, April 19: You occasionally fall into the trap of grudge-holding which isn't really worthy of your clearheaded sign. Today it's impossible to hang on to it any longer as someone comes back and extends a hand. The two of you shake and resolve to stick together in the future. You are relieved.

Friday, April 20: MOON IN CAPRICORN. Your spirits take a swift upward turn as the moon moves into your sign. You feel very outgoing, and should dress the part because new and interesting contacts are a distinct possibility today. Trust your first impressions of people because they are bound to be accurate today.

Saturday, April 21: You are seeing things in such a bright light that you even dredge up an old idea and make it brand new again. It sparkles, and so do you as you show off your delightful sense of humor. You are in a talkative mood, and ask a lot more questions of others than you normally do. People generally like it, you know.

Sunday, April 22: This is self-improvement day, and you take stock of yourself and what you have. You are not the slightest bit put off when someone offers you some constructive criticism; your self-confidence is pretty solid now. An annoying job you've been avoiding is easy to push off. The day's lucky number is 4.

Monday, April 23: You may have to go on a "dig" today and the buried treasure is information you need. Don't be afraid to lean on some people who are key to your search; keep jabbing away until they come up with the answers. You are finally able to put it all together so it makes sense, and you are satisfied.

Tuesday, April 24: You are able to convince others to do it your way and the result is profitable for all. It gives you a reason to congratulate yourself by indulging in some good music and a harmonious domestic atmosphere. You are truly king or queen in your own castle.

Wednesday, April 25: The world is very much with you today, and you may not like having to spend so much time filling people in. Give up your privacy for the day, and keep a sharp eye on messages that come in. Some may have a hidden clue. Someone wants to meet in secret, and you reluctantly agree. The number 7 could be a winner today.

Thursday, April 26: You might be off in a cloud of dust today as a trip suddenly becomes urgent; don't be mysterious about your whereabouts. Explain that this trip is necessary to tie up loose ends you don't want to leave dangling any longer. It's to everyone's benefit, as you are able to point out.

Friday, April 27: The best thing for you is to occasionally meet people who are real risk-takers. You come face to face with someone like that today and it inspires you to resolve to take the initiative more often. One-on-one contact with this person is very useful in taking stock of your plus and minus factors.

Saturday, April 28: Yesterday's experience goes a long way in promoting your mellow mood today. Family relations are quite harmonious—particularly with your mate or partner. Inside you are coming up with some creative concepts; you should share them with others—particularly children.

Sunday, April 29: You are not normally impulsive, so when you get an urge to act today, temper it in your

120

usual way. There are no easy answers or shortcuts to getting what you want. Listen to a very solid citizen who has a plan that is practically airtight. Your logic tells you he or she is the one to take your lead from.

Monday, April 30: How many people can you give a piece of your time to? Ration out your good will and good humor so you don't lose any of it. Accept some invitations to appear in person, but give others short shrift. You love a good time, but you know you can get quite strung out when you spread yourself too thin.

May 1984

Astronote to Capricorn: Mother's Day comes in May, and May is the traditional month for the celebration of women. For the Capricorn woman, "tradition" is an important word. Home, roots, family history—all figure high on her list of values. In fact, the man who marries a Capricorn woman had better make sure he is as compatible with her family as he is with her. The home she makes with her husband will be invested with all her love and devotion—but a lot of money is also part of the picture. While it is not true to say that Capricorn women always marry for wealth, material security for them is a necessity. Many Capricorn women seek it for themselves in the world of profession and career, and most of them really make it. That does not preclude marriage, however, because isn't marriage the traditional thing for women to do by a certain age? Even in our enlightened society the Capricorn woman regards a husband as something she cannot live without. And no matter how much money she makes, she will regard her mate not only as prime provider but as master accountant of the household. She will work shoulder to shoulder with him to keep hearth and home running smoothly—and efficiently, particularly cost-efficiently.

The Capricorn woman is an excellent manager—of both people and money—and is serious about her work, both in and out of the home. She may appear the most frivolous and/or sexy of creatures, but she will always know what she is doing and when dinner is to be on the table. She will choose a mate who shares her love of lavish entertaining and her desire to have the "best of everything." It has been said that the Capricorn woman does not necessarily want to keep up with the Joneses—she wants to be ahead of them. She will stick with the conventional even in her choice of decor and food, however; only when something has been accepted into the mainstream will she introduce it into her own scheme of things.

The Capricorn female invests so much love and devotion into her marriage and family that her children are likely to be "the best" as well. That is, if good manners, clean clothes, and absolute adherence to the rules are used as the measures. The children of a Capricorn mother may wish from time to time that she would loosen up, but they will never want for her attention. She is achievement-oriented, so she will oversee their mental and physical development and keep alert to any possible early warnings of deficiency. Woe to the child who brings home a mediocre report card. She will not punish, but she will lecture. No matter what her faults, the Capricorn female makes an exemplary wife and mother. Like the things she likes to collect, she will be valuable and an adornment to the household.

Tuesday, May 1: What looks like a pretty messy situation really has more to it than appears. The facts you have are a bit sketchy, to say the least, but it's worth your while to fill in the blanks. You will feel easier about taking the risk involved, and see that it's a shoo-in for success.

Wednesday, May 2: Today you have the opposite problem; you may get so carried away with optimism and enthusiasm that you can't see the pitfalls. Sure, you feel good because you've got a load off your mind, but don't get too frisky with this one. Probe for all the answers you need.

Thursday, May 3: Things are calming down quite a bit; in fact you may feel bored. Use the time to get more organized; you've been backsliding more than is usual for you. Discipline is good for everyone—including you. Give yourself "Brownie points" by lending a helping hand to others.

Friday, May 4: You may feel as if you are going bananas with the amount of work you've got and the demands that keep coming in. Take a deep breath and relax; you can handle it all if you don't panic. A report you have to concentrate on is extremely important to your standing; accept the help of someone who may offer it rather shyly.

Saturday, May 5: The get-organized movement you join in at home today is light stuff compared with yesterday. Enjoy working together with family members toward the greater good of all. The improvements you make may not be huge ones, but everybody looks at them and you in admiration.

Sunday, May 6: Temper, temper, temper! Don't react in anger when someone tries to force you into a decision you aren't ready to make. Just insist on more time—part of which should be spent comparing notes with your opposite number. Together you can decide on the direction you want to go. The number 7 is a good one today.

Monday, May 7: You are usually pretty comfortable in the role of boss, but today you may be doling out work to some temporarily temperamental people. Keep your cool. Someone has a secret to tell you that will rather amaze you—and give you a clue as to how to act. Someone special of the opposite sex has his or her eye on you.

Tuesday, May 8: There's somebody you can't quite make out—but would like very much to know. Today you get the chance to move in, and it proves very interesting. Cultivate this relationship. You may be called on to fill in a group of people on some data. Take a really fresh approach. Everyone will appreciate it.

Wednesday, May 9: You are on top of the heap today and have a fabulous opportunity to make an unforgettable impression. Don't blow it by being too heavy-handed; a touch of humor will be much more appreciated and demonstrate your originality. Watch out for someone who is almost overcome with jealousy; you can make him or her laugh it off if you approach it right.

Thursday, May 10: You are right to lift your mind to higher thoughts today; sometimes you can get overly involved in things that really do not matter. You will gain insight into what your true values are, and it will aid you when you return to the world of getting and spending.

Friday, May 11: With your ability to exhibit grace under pressure you cheer everyone on today. The light touch is just what's needed for the morale of all. Stress to everyone that it's quality and not quantity that counts in the long run—and on the bottom line. The day's lucky number is 3.

Saturday, May 12: You are on really firm ground in a discussion today because you know the basics better than anyone in this matter. Someone may try to test you, but you come out a winner when you demonstrate your in-depth understanding. Someone more objective is willing to provide information you can use.

Sunday, May 13: Be a freethinker today; toss out some outworn ideas about how things should be done and do them a new way. Take some time out to start that day-by-day personal record. Don't call it a diary, though; call it your journal and record your thoughts. You will be surprised at how useful the technique can be.

Monday, May 14: You experience a bit of a conflict between home and work today; something's got to give. You work it out by making both sides make an adjustment. Harmony reigns at home as a result, and that's the most important thing to you. Today's important number is 6.

Tuesday, May 15: Yesterday's experience leads you to some personal evaluating today; try to get away and be alone. As you focus on current hopes and dreams for tomorrow, you get a clear vision of what it's all about. It's almost a spiritual feeling, and you feel as if a weight has been lifted off you. Talk about it to a Pisces person who will understand.

Mid-month memo to Capricorn: A Capricorn woman can be rather hard to please; that's why finding an appropriate gift can be such a chore that it takes the feeling out of the gesture. Sure, an expensive pair of earrings will be appreciated, but she's likely to have similar ones already. Yes, that "state of the art" stereo would look and sound great in her living room—but the "old" one hasn't been around that long. Paradoxically, the Capricorn woman has certain thrifty instincts. One of the reasons she buys the best is so it will last. So the giver must be very creative when selecting a gift for the Capricorn woman; extra effort will be very meaningful to her. For instance, one could arrange to have her family genealogy done to satisfy her sense of history. Comb old bookstores for a rare first edition of her favorite author. Subscribe to a magazine that caters to a special interest like art or antiques. Whatever it is, she will enjoy it all the more if she can tell her other friends about how much her wonderful husband/lover/friend does for her.

Wednesday, May 16: MOON IN CAPRICORN. You are far from pensive today; the watchword is "action." As you wheel and deal about money and power, you are amazed to find that a tough competitor is a member of the opposite sex. That puts an even more interesting complexion on things. Inside you realize you will have to give up a little in order to gain.

Thursday, May 17: You are practically forced to think big today; what you are dealing with requires an attitude adjustment toward a much larger frame of reference. You are not only up to it, you love it—as you love being involved in behind-the-scenes activity. Remember your principles and don't compromise integrity.

Friday, May 18: You don't exactly need top hat and tails, but do dress up a bit today and prepare yourself to be on-stage. Whatever you are involved in today totally involves you and people are drawn to you by the energy you give off. Be a little careful about overdoing physically; you could wear yourself out.

Saturday, May 19: It is good to retire from the hustle and bustle of the week and spend some quiet time with a very compassionate person. She—and it is most likely a she—has an absolutely healing effect on your jangled nerves and jarred senses. You learn how to relax a little and heal yourself.

Sunday, May 20: It looks as if you will be of two minds today; so try to get your act together and know where you are going before you take a step. You may have to do some routine visiting and running around, but don't take any major action until your head is clearer. The lucky number is 3.

Monday, May 21: Basic resources must be called into play in order to deal with some brass tacks problems that need nailing down. You are up to it, and even able to see where savings can be made. Put your conservative cap on today for best results. There's no room for impulsive action. The number 4 is important today.

Tuesday, May 22: If you are ultra-tactful in a note you write today, you stand a good chance of recouping an old debt that is owed you. It's sticky business, but not impossible. A brother or sister may be in the picture and may introduce an interesting new individual who takes an interest in you.

Wednesday, May 23: You take a big step and make with confidence today; your judgment is keen and your momentum strong. As you move ahead, you do it in the spirit of the greatest good for the greatest number—which, of course, includes family. You are able to ignore the superficialities.

Thursday, May 24: You want absolutely everything to be open and aboveboard today—demand of others the same definition of terms that you insist on for yourself; don't let them gloss things over. It's too important not to get total disclosure. When you are finally filled in on the whole story, you are not too pleased that some have been deceptive.

Friday, May 25: All your instincts for helping others are stimulated today; someone you really care about needs your protection and your advice. Giving it makes you feel virtuous, and spurs you to be very responsible in another area of things. By day's end you have nicely cemented two relationships.

Saturday, May 26: Roots and traditions are high on the list of your interests today. Working along with someone equally enthusiastic, you complete a job that makes home and hearth a much warmer place. With such basic values at the top of your mind, it is easy to persuade you to go along with a worthy cause.

Sunday, May 27: A rather flamboyant person has a great effect on you today; his or her showmanship is so impressive you decide to hop on the bandwagon. You're ready for a new start, and your energy level is pretty high. You can afford to be a little adventurous because matters of money and property are secure.

Monday, May 28: You want to entertain and be entertained today; you are really in the mood for excitement. You can easily generate some, but be prudent with your time and energy. A tendency to excess is indicated, and even sensible you could fall victim to it. The lucky number is 11.

Tuesday, May 29: Once again you must pace yourself; you may be involved in a whirlwind of social activity. Take a leaf from the book of someone who is able to enjoy life immensely without losing a bit of cool. Show your originality at a gathering where you may be called on to do a number.

Wednesday, May 30: You feel like a cat on a hot tin roof; nothing drives you wilder than having to wait. In the meantime you could do some ground work to clear the decks for the action that is coming soon. Get your mind on things by having a give-and-take conversation with someone older and wiser than you. It will make you see how you can increase your options.

Thursday, May 31: The air clears today and you can see ahead; what you spot are some interesting changes. They may start today as you interact with a group of stimulating people. Suddenly something that's been obscure becomes perfectly obvious. Don't kick yourself for not having seen it before. Act on it now.

June 1984

Astronote to Capricorn: Father's Day is the month's biggest holiday, which makes it a good time to see how the Capricorn male performs in the role of husband and father.

One of the tragic figures of the zodiac is the Capricorn man who sacrifices home and family to his overriding need to be successful. What is most ironic is that the Capricorn man who finds his family has deserted him has really been so busy because he has been making money for their pleasure and comfort. But sometimes no amount of material things can compensate for the absenteeism of the ambitious Capricorn male. It may only be mental business trips that he takes, but they are often too frequent in terms of loneliness for his wife and children. Luckier Capricorn men are able to balance out their devotion to career and duty with their love of family. Sometimes they prove to be those Capricorns who choose to marry late—late enough so that their do-or-die business days are over. Sometimes they are simply the more sensitive men of the sign who observe building tension and head it off at the pass by giving their family their due.

When he is in residence, both physically and mentally, the Capricorn man runs the risk of casting a pall over the household by being too demanding. After all, he picked this woman as carefully as he would an investment opportunity. And both are likely to be "blue chip" choices made both for their good looks and ability to perform. The wife of the Capricorn knows he can't stand anything shoddy, so she will tend to hide imperfections from his eyes—such as the rug that got whisked off to the cleaners when the family dog broke training. She will protect her children as carefully as she protects her husband.

The Capricorn father is possibly the strictest in the zodiac, and the tendency really comes from his penchant for tradition and convention. If they hear it once in their lifetimes the children of a Capricorn father will hear it a thousand times: "They didn't do things like that in my day." The teenage years are particularly precarious for children in a Capricorn-father household. It is at this point that the mother may hvae to be particularly inventive if she is to let her children keep up with the social circle of their peers.

The Capricorn father can be great, however. He's particularly understanding when his children just *must* have something. He will not spoil them by lavishing them with meaningless gifts—but he will indulge their passions for certain possessions. The biggest thrill the children of Capricorn fathers can get is getting dad to break down and laugh. He does when it is appropriate, and that is a tribute to his humanity and understanding of the people he loves.

Friday, June 1: There's a lot you can capitalize on today—one is your open lines of communication with some people in a position to advertise your cause. Be very clear about the legal rights of everyone involved in a sticky situation, which may involve what belongs to whom. The days's important number is 3.

Saturday, June 2: Patience is a virtue you may have to exhibit in spades today; there is a lot of dissension in the ranks. Talk to someone who knows the ropes and can give you some clues about how to deal with things. At least there are some pretty reasonable people in the wings who are willing to help.

Sunday, June 3: You've been so distracted the past few days you really have neglected someone who does not like being neglected. He or she may require some special wooing and winning. You've been through this before so you've got a pretty good idea of which buttons to push to get the response you want. That's not being cynical; that's just being practical.

Monday, June 4: Some found money drops into your lap today. It's really your due from an old debt, but in effect it is manna from heaven. You feel like using it to add nice touches to your place; go ahead and splurge. You're entitled. Meanwhile you have a deal going which may turn a hobby into a profitable enterprise. Things are looking good.

Tuesday, June 5: Your nerves may be a bit on edge today. Your best course is to retire from the fray and find a quiet spot where you can hide and think. Try to give priorities to your important worries, and drop a lot of the small ones. The world will not fall apart if you do not do everything perfectly. The lucky number is 7.

Wednesday, June 6: Get back in the mainstream today, but ease in rather than plunge. Steady as she goes should be your watchword today. Spend your time putting things in order; it will make you feel a lot less disorganized. You are sometimes too demanding of yourself when it comes to doing things the right way. Someone not too nearby checks in with a pleasant message that makes you feel a lot better.

Thursday, June 7: You are very much back on the track now—so much that an idea you had buried surfaces again and you can see its possibilities. A lot of your sureness about it is pure intuition, but rest assured it is sound. Look ahead with confidence now; there's not much that can daunt you.

Friday, June 8: This is a high visibility day. Even if you don't seek it you will find that you stand out from the crowd. It forces you to be your old assertive self. Everybody approves, including your peers who are glad to see you back in your old form. For more good things try your luck with number 1.

Saturday, June 9: Along with a friend—a rather inventive one—you get involved in something off the beaten track for you. You find you love the diversion, and that being a bit unorthodox doesn't really bother you at all. In fact, you are just dying to share what you learn with friends, children, and others.

Sunday, June 10: You are really having a ball this weekend. Today you show off your new talent to a bunch of people who think it's great and look at you in a new way. They love your sense of humor, too; you owe a lot of your new popularity to someone who's given you tips about how to show off your positive side. It may just be a Sagitarrian.

Monday, June 11: Something that's been standing in your way just seems to vanish; there's a big wide road ahead—and it's open for you. You feel that your dreams are about to come true and it puts you in a very romantic mood. Use it to win someone over to your cause permanently. The number 4 may help.

Tuesday, June 12: You are brought back to reality abruptly today when you realize someone is trying to make a patsy of you. One thing you cannot stand is when people think they can pull the wool over your penetrating eyes. Give him or her your famous I-want-the-answers look and you will be amazed at how quickly you get a straight story.

Wednesday, June 13: You have to let your mate or partner know that a certain pattern has to be broken. It may require an adjustment on the home scene, but you both owe it to yourselves to have a little more peace and quiet. With your public relations skills, you should be able to smooth over the waters and soon nobody will even remember what it was like before.

Thursday, June 14: MOON IN CAPRICORN. Nobody but nobody can get a free ride with you today. Your sense of self is at a high as the moon moves into your sign. Your confidence and feeling of having it "together" gains you a lot of points—and some admiring glances. You are able to see things for what they are and that may disconcert some people who thought you were more gullible.

Friday, June 15: You've never been more ready to take on a challenge—no matter how much time and energy may be required. In fact, you virtually jump at the chance to grab responsibility and thereby call some good attention to yourself. Another Capricorn may be involved. The day's hot number is 7.

Mid-month memo to Capricorn: What in the world can one give a Capricorn man? He's often the proverbial man who has everything. Not that he is totally self-indulgent; his tendency to be so well-equipped comes from his desire to demonstrate that he is a well-heeled, solid citizen. There is a clue in his nature to the kind of gifts he will appreciate, however. It's got to be a hard-headed purchase that shows you know true value—which is quite another thing from price. In fact, gift-givers are better off leaving the price tag on their gift to the male Capricorn—if it will demonstrate that they got a lot for their money. Like the Capricorn woman, the male of the species enjoys showing off how much his family and friends think of him. One gift that serves a lot of good purposes for him is a family portrait. One copy should be small enough so he can carry it around with him and proudly show people his most precious possessions.

Saturday, June 16: A mellow mood is upon you and you feel inclined to stretch your tastes in the area of art and music. You have a sense of what is good, but you want to go beyond that. In your heart you believe you have some talent; don't be afraid to test yourself. You can gain a lot of personal satisfaction from the effort.

Sunday, June 17: Today it is your more material resources that preoccupy your thoughts. Yes, you can take a firmer hold on your financial destiny if you hold on to the courage of your convictions about the worth of certain things. Your dynamic attitude is impressive to a member of the opposite sex.

Monday, June 18: You may be a bit preachy today, but what you talk about is of fascination to others. You've got a good handle on what is coming and—like most people—your friends want to share your vision. The real material possibilities are a ways off, but you are able to convince people of the potential.

Tuesday, June 19: If you don't watch it you could easily wind up this day totally strung out. Your mind is working at full speed and your body wants to keep up. You would be wise to make a sensible schedule and stick to it. Because you are so distracted by all the activity, be sure to protect your valuables and hang on to things so you don't leave them behind in your haste.

Wednesday, June 20: A rather niggling project comes your way today, and it involves going over some ground you have already covered. Though it's a drag, don't give in to the temptation to turn it over to someone else. You started this thing and it's up to you to finish it. To lighten your mood, try your luck with number 4.

Thursday, June 21: If your expectations are high today, you will not be disappointed. First, some confirmations

133

you've been waiting for come by mail or phone. Next, you hook up with just the right person to help you get things moving. All in all, you feel a lot more secure than you did earlier. You may not be aware of it, but some interesting eyes have been on you today.

Friday, June 22: A minor but disconcerting ripple in the domestic calm has been bugging you of late. Today the waters are smoothed over; you feel just great about it—especially when someone gives you something that's a real token of his or her affection. You are never at your best when the home scene is not calm; so this development delights you.

Saturday, June 23: An idea or answer comes to you out of the blue and makes you realize you are going down the right road—no matter what others say. Ignore your slight apprehensions and rest assured you are on the right track. You can gain a big advantage by keeping your own counsel until the moment is exactly right. When you spring your surprise attack you gain a big advantage.

Sunday, June 24: This is a day to devote yourself to pleasure pursuits. The things you get involved in bring you closer to someone you've been wanting to know. The relationship is likely to blossom and you are likely to go out on a limb and promise your emotional backing. It's a risk you should take.

Monday, June 25: Again your pleasure and that of others take priority. Today the accent is on the mental rather than the physical; it's a great day to read a good book or take in a recommended movie or play. The most important thing is that you feel free to do what you please. Your helping qualities are brought to the fore as well when you counsel someone about a personal health matter.

Tuesday, June 26: You are fed up to the teeth with people at the top who are about as dynamic as a wet noodle. Instead of feeling frustrated about the situation, today you decide to grab the reins and take the initiative. You are surprised at the warm welcome you get and the thanks that co-workers give you for having the guts to do something.

Wednesday, June 27: Your vision is very sharp today. What you observe makes it obvious to you which course to choose. It's a conservative one and it may involve persuading others to economize. Put your house in order without criticizing anyone; you will get far better cooperation with a pleasant attitude. The number 2 will be useful.

Thursday, June 28: You find you are more than a bit bored with the same old routine and resolve to get out of your rut. Some big ideas which require substantial reading and research may be a bit more than your partner wants to handle. Tone things down to a level where you both can enjoy yourselves.

Friday, June 29: That's better! Today you streamline your proposed projects so they are manageable for everyone. You've devised a plan for throwing out the old to make room for the new, and it makes a lot of sense—especially when you portion out the responsibility fairly. Don't falter and leave things half done; be confident that the result you want can be accomplished.

Saturday, June 30: You are the one who makes others think fast today. You have a lot to find out and not much time to do it. Keep a sharp lookout for someone who may be trying to gull you. There's a minor risk involved in what you want to do, but if you don't fall asleep at the switch you'll come through with flying colors.

July 1984

Astronote to Capricorn: It's pretty hard to thwart a Capricorn, but even this sturdy sign has times when obstacles seem almost impossible to hurdle. This month, when the sun is in the sign of your opposite number,

Cancer, you may encounter more frustrations than usual. In a sense, your sun is at its yearly low point. Take the opportunity to observe how you deal with opposition, Capricorn; it may tell you a great deal more about yourself than you know.

Capricorn is the zodiac sign that has a very strong sense of self. Put another way, Capricorn has a pretty big ego. Certain other astrological factors may temper this tendency, but deep down in every Capricorn you will find the conviction that he or she is "the best." What happens, then, when Capricorn can't control the situation and is shunted aside? Sometimes it's not a pretty sight to behold. When somebody or something blocks Capricorn's well-thought-out path, he or she can become downright cruel. It isn't as venomous as Scorpio's lashing out can be, but it is equally as devastating. Capricorn's cruelty can take the form of biting, acid sarcasm which cuts to the quick—or more subtle forms such as pretending others simply do not exist or that they are pariahs.

As is usually the case with normal human beings, most of the time Capricorn is suffering as badly as the other party. However, to get things back on the track, the others will have to make the first move. Usually, Capricorn is carved out of stone and that makes the sign pretty static when it comes to making gestures. The quickest way to melt his or her heart and effect a reconciliation is with a little flattery.

Sunday, July 1: You feel inclined to pull in your horns today and do some defensive accounting. Your motive is to build up your financial resources so that you will be on a more solid foundation. On the lighter side, don't pass up the opportunity to do something truly unusual; the person who asks is so inventive you are assured of a good time.

Monday, July 2: There's an undercurrent of passionate involvement today; you are finding yourself more and more in the grip of a relationship. Be sure it is what you want. It doesn't distract you from the work at hand, however, where you are able to make a great showing and get some tangible playback.

Tuesday, July 3: Aha, now you see! You are elated when you finally understand a complicated subject; it feels good to get it. On the domestic scene, you finish off some improvements; everyone compliments your efforts. The number 6 is important today.

Wednesday, July 4: You've got a sneaky suspicion something is going on that you ought to know about. It isn't paranoia, you discover, when you talk to someone who is willing to clue you in. Now you know the right course is to lay back and wait. It bugs you to have to pretend you don't know what's going on.

Thursday, July 5: Don't get so carried away by being able to move ahead that you drop some stitches! You're in the catbird seat today, but you could jeopardize your lead by being careless. Remember, you are not in this alone and that there are others depending on you. A compatible Cancer is a big help.

Friday, July 6: Make a big effort to get something finished today; you will be glad when it's no longer hanging over your head. Respond positively when you are asked to explain a rather complicated matter to some people you work with; they count on your being able to see the big picture. A charitable urge comes over you and you convince others to go along in a humanitarian venture.

Saturday, July 7: You are touched and amused when some friendly characters pull off a stunt that nets you something you've been wishing for. Your energy level is high and you jump at the chance to do something a little different and daring. The people who get you out and around are good ones to pal with.

Sunday, July 8: This is a mighty sociable weekend; don't crowd your schedule so much that you neglect to do what you promised yourself you would do. That means get in there and clear the decks for action. Clutter will only clutter your mind when you get down to business later on.

Monday, July 9: It's a good thing you know how to keep your mouth shut, because if you tip your hand too early you run the risk of messing up a long-range scheme. People will know soon enough. Someone you like gives you something cute and you are touched by the gesture. Like most people, you love being surprised—be sure you get that across to the giver.

Tuesday, July 10: Check, check, and recheck. It's a bore but it's necessary if you intend to find something solid enough to take a stand on. There is someone who could give you a tip; even though he or she would prefer to be a silent partner. Give the person a call and see if there's a willingness to cooperate. Give another call to someone who's confined at home or in the hospital.

Wednesday, July 11: MOON IN CAPRICORN. You get that extra burst of energy the moon in your sign can give. Trust yourself when you decide to act; this is not impulsiveness but a real perception that the time is now! Too much time has been spent on airy-fairy schemes; this is reality. Others are impressed with your decisiveness and tell you so.

Thursday, July 12: Today you feel very inclined to reach out to people, and the first place you do it is at home. The reaction is warm and you are pleased that you are able to make someone feel comfortable. Your helping sense is so in tune today that you keep spreading good things wherever you do. The number 6 will prove a winner.

Friday, July 13: Who's in charge here? You, and don't let anyone make any mistake about it. Your decisiveness leads you to take a firm stand and it is a winning stance. You are helped when a murky situation suddenly becomes clear as crystal. There's nothing anyone can say now that will make you change your mind.

Saturday, July 14: It's going to cost you some time, but that's about all, so you should rejoice that your fond wish will soon come true. Now that you can see it within your reach, you are able to share your secret with a few others. Someone—possibly a fellow Capricorn—encourages you with his or her vote of confidence.

Sunday, July 15: The good thing about getting in on the ground floor is that there's nowhere to go but up! That's the situation you find yourself in today, and it makes you optimistic for the future. It's going to take some hard work and a lot of careful planning, but this is one deal you feel lucky to be in on.

Mid-month memo to Capricorn: As you evaluate yourself this month, Capricorn, you should focus on your real strengths—some of which you tend to ignore or undervalue because they are second nature to you. One is dependability. Most Capricorns, by the time youth is past, have grown into the label old reliable. Even as children, Capricorns do not usually need a lot of prodding to perform their duties. To some of you the reputation for dependability begins to stick in your throat and you wish someone would say something *else* nice about you. Don't sell yourself short; it is an extremely lovable characteristic. In any relationship the element of trust figures big and you always come out strong in that department. The fact that you can be counted upon is also a tremendous factor to Capricorn's success in the business and professional worlds. Silently and swiftly, Capricorn does what has to be done; as egotistical as he or she may be, Capricorn doesn't have to be told how wonderful he or she is just for doing what is expected.

Monday, July 16: It's going to be a little difficult, but you've got to keep the details of your new enterprise under wraps for now. However, the feeling of security makes you able to assert yourself in another area. For fun, you pull off a surprise that delights someone else—and amuses you as well. The day's lucky number is 1.

Tuesday, July 17: You may very well run into a rather unsettling situation today, but don't let it throw you. Your best course is not to exhibit any anxiety, but to calmly and cooly collect all the facts and retire into a corner to analyze them. Tell others you are concerned, but as objectively as possible.

Wednesday, July 18: You feel a lot better with yesterday's problem out of the way, and are more than ready for a change—and some fun. It runs right into you in the form of a rather fascinating person. He or she likes a lot of the same things you do so there's plenty to talk about. A Gemini may give you competition, however. The number 3 will be significant.

Thursday, July 19: Things get back on a more routine track today and it is comfortable for you. You dig in to get some things done, but are interrupted when some property matters arise that must be settled. You are not in the mood, but resign yourself that you have to deal with them.

Friday, July 20: You are noted for appearing to be the strong, silent type, regardless of your sex. You get to display some of that poise today when you are called upon to demonstrate your efficiency under fire. It's a piece of cake for you, and someone of the opposite sex not only notices but lets you know he or she is impressed.

Saturday, July 21: This is a sharing day. You find you get even more pleasure out of a special interest when others work along with you. There's an artistic element in whatever you do, whether painting, playing music, working on a craft—or even cooking. All involved get a little sentimental about how nice you are to each other.

Sunday, July 22: Today you have another emotional experience, but of a very different kind. Introspection leads to a feeling that is almost psychic. Your sense of contact with others is heightened, and you come out of it determined that you will help others as much as possible. A Pisces person may be the one you share your thoughts with.

Monday, July 23: There's a Mexican standoff between you and a loved one today; you can't both get what you want. The issue is not a vital one, so you go ahead and make the decision. The outing you take charge of turns out to be a delightful experience for everyone involved—and your pushiness is vindicated.

Tuesday, July 24: You are so enthusiastic about a cause and so eager to help that you run the risk of overdoing things today. Your charitable feelings are very worthy ones, but you might do better staying close to home base and communicating the appeal by telephone. You are persuasive enough to get others involved, too.

Wednesday, July 25: You've been talking and thinking about it long enough; today you take the plunge into an exercise-for-health program. You are so pleased with yourself for making this new start in a good direction that you decide to give yourself a treat; just don't overspend.

Thursday, July 26: Someone wants to make a contract with you today; don't go whole hog. By a few fancy maneuvers you can agree in principle but not get locked in. The person who offers the deal makes an emotional appeal for wholehearted agreement. You are not ready to go that far. The important number today is 11.

Friday, July 27: You display such a marvelous and refreshing sense of humor today that you give a very bubbly person a run for his or her money. Your optimism and lighthearted mood are catching wherever you go. Just don't get so carried away you get sloppy with a matter that requires close attention.

141

Saturday, July 28: It's a drag to have a deal with something you thought was over and done with. When it surfaces you realize you're the only one who can get involved; in this case delegating simply doesn't work. Someone confides in you by telling you of a secret romantic interest and you are a bit embarrassed.

Sunday, July 29: It's up to you to protect something that belongs to someone else, and you take your charge seriously. That's why you get rather insistent when some evasive people dance around the subject; you are after a straight story and you won't settle for anything less. The number 5 is significant.

Monday, July 30: There's been a bit of distance between you and your mate recently. You are able to reestablish contact and come close together again. Both of you are relieved that the tension is over. Now you can start to plan for a trip that doesn't seem like such a far-off possibility any longer.

Tuesday July 31: You are able to keep your perspective today even though all is not a bed of roses. Suddenly the difficulties seem minor in the light of what is really important to you. You adopt a philosophical attitude and resolve not to let anything get you down. The lucky number is 7.

August 1984

Astronote to Capricorn: If you know your rising sign you know a lot more about your astrological profile than most people. The phrase is probably the most confusing one in the astrologer's vocabulary. Simply put, your rising sign is determined by the clock time at your moment of birth. Whatever the hour, your rising sign is the one that was on the eastern horizon at that time—the point you would touch if you extended your left hand to the extreme left from your birthplace. Why is it important? The rising sign is powerful because it tends to throw a cover over your sun sign. In our existence on earth, we are meant to act out our sun sign—but our rising sign goes everywhere we go and is often how others see us rather than how we think we appear. You can determine your rising sign from the chart on pages 69–70 if you know your birth time within one hour. Here's how the various rising signs act when they are the cover for Capricorn:

Capricorn sun sign with Aries rising: You are one tough customer. You may try to dominate every situation you walk into and have quite a bit less of the famous Capricorn reserve. Try not to come on so strong.

Capricorn sun sign with Taurus rising: You have a tendency to make a great show of your material well-being. On the other hand, you are rather soft and approachable for a Capricorn.

Capricorn sun sign with Gemini rising: This is the Capricorn who will know the names of everyone in the room within ten seconds after entering it. You are genial and personable and a little more talkative than other Capricorns.

Capricorn sun sign with Cancer rising: At times, you may come off as a real sad sack. The impression people get is that you are in terrible pain. Try putting on a big smile when going into new situations.

Capricorn sun sign with Leo rising: This makes for a rather flashy character with a warm handshake and a hearty grin. It also makes for an impossible egotist. You are not the only one who deserves attention.

Capricorn sun sign with Virgo rising: You may wonder why people hardly seem to notice you and you may get rather annoyed. The problem with this retiring combination is that you are never the one to make the first move.

Capricorn sun sign with Libra rising: It's possible that you come off as rather haughty at best and a terrible snob at worst. You are friendly, but it is little comfort to those who prefer a warmer response.

Capricorn sun sign with Scorpio rising: You may stop traffic when you come on scene because you appear so impressively in control. Don't give in to the opportunity handed you to dominate everybody and everything.

Capricorn sun sign with Sagittarius rising: Here is a real politician. You are so busy trying to figure out who is important and who you can impress that you may not have any fun at all.

Capricorn sun sign with Capricorn rising: What you see is what you get: a rather reserved individual who isn't really shy but you need some coaxing to display your considerable intelligence.

Capricorn sun sign with Aquarius rising: You can seem downright cold, and if you open up with your acid sense of humor you may find that people retreat to more genial types.

Capricorn sun sign with Pisces rising: What a surprise people get when they discover you are not at all the pushover you appear. It's a great disguise, however, because you gain people's confidence rather quickly.

Wednesday, August 1: You have to turn on a dime today when something occurs that requires instantaneous action. This is one time it helps to have clout, and your ability to cut through red tape shows you do. There's still a warm feeling generated by a recent reconciliation with your mate or romantic partner.

Thursday, August 2: A niggling problem is put behind and you are able to turn your attention to higher things. Though not a professional critic, you are an art lover, and today you indulge that interest along with a friend who shares it. He or she could possibly be a Taurus and offers you new insights which give you greater appreciation.

Friday, August 3: You've been feeling some dissatisfaction recently, and today you decide to lay it to rest. The route you choose is to perfect some areas of your life that are less than organized. Some near and dear friends are very willing to help because they, too, would like to see you serene.

Saturday, August 4: This is no laid-back Saturday. First crack out of the box you have to take some decisive action in a matter where you hold the responsibility. You whip everyone into shape with your keen sense of organization, and a project goes off smoothly. In the course of it, you impress someone with your abilities and he or she becomes a closer pal.

Sunday, August 5: Yesterday's experience makes you sit back and contemplate your own strengths and weaknesses today. As you take inventory, you realize you've got more to offer than you thought. You decide to get involved in a good cause where help is needed. Today's big number is 9.

Monday, August 6: Today you take the "new you" out into the world. You are determined to leave old ideas and old self-images behind and strike out on a whole new path. It may just be that you come on too strong, however, because there is someone who is a bit confused by your vehemence. Cool it a bit; you can get what you want without overdoing.

Tuesday, August 7: You are quite a bit calmer today and aware you must do some groundwork first. Spend the day putting some pieces together and making a game plan. You may have to say "no" to a tempting invitation, but you know how important your new resolutions are. The day's lucky number is 2.

Wednesday, August 8: MOON IN CAPRICORN. Now you can play a little because your mind is clearer about

145

what you want and how you intend to go about getting it. Some playmates are dying to have you join them in an amusing adventure. They insist it wouldn't work without you. Isn't it nice to have that kind of magnetic personality?

Thursday, August 9: Your work is cut out for you today and it requires quite a bit of concentration. No sweat, however, since you are feeling both energetic and confident. Some good buddies—possibly a Leo and an Aquarius—are so much fun to work along with that the time just flies.

— Friday, August 10: A rather significant change seems to be right at hand; it could affect your whole living arrangement and/or love life. The issue seems to be personal possessions—or at least a matter of personal values. It is possible that you decide upon a long-term plan and take the first step now.

Saturday, August 11: You have an irresistible urge to turn everything upside down and redo it. Your "new broom fever" affects the whole household and everybody pitches in to refinish, refurbish, and renew. The surroundings end up being a lot brighter, and a good time is had by all. The winning number today is 6.

Sunday, August 12: Today most of your activity is focused inward, and you actually are more comfortable alone than with others. You decide you've got to chuck some old ideas along with other debris in order to get your life on the right track. Some insights you uncover can be classified as "spiritual."

Monday, August 13: You get down to serious business today. Some time, effort, and interest you invested in the past come back to you today in the form of an excellent deal. Property may be involved. It is easy for you to decide what to do, and you are confident you made the right choice.

Tuesday, August 14: Far away but not forgotten, someone important reenters your life today. A good chat you have with him or her makes you realize you are not alone in reassessing your life at this point. It makes you even more determined to complete your personal inventory and get your act together.

Wednesday, August 15: The best way to advance your interests today is to take someone by surprise. Caught off-guard, he or she will be much more vulnerable to your request. You've got to be assertive as well, however, because what you are asking for is a little unorthodox. An older person draws closer to you and you are glad the relationship is getting better.

Mid-month memo to Capricorn: Regardless of your rising sign, there is a commonly acknowledged trait of Capricorn that really holds true for virtually all members of the sign. That is the tendency to be a climber. But is that all bad? Does it necessarily mean that Capricorn will push others aside to rise on the social or career ladder? No. There are many Capricorns who do not allow their deep-seated need to achieve to interfere with their humanity. They take their clue from the mountain goat that is the famous Capricorn symbol. He or she can jump nimbly from crag to crag in the upward climb and leave plenty of room for others to find their own way. The upwardly mobile Capricorn will not always extend a helping hand to those who are slower. Capricorn's motto is everyone for him- or herself, however. The Capricorn rarely asks for help or special privileges and expects the same independence of everyone else. Without fanfare, Capricorn will ascend the mountain and be waiting for the others when they arrive.

Thursday, August 16: Don't be extravagant with anything today, including your energy. Take it slow and easy and concentrate on battening down the hatches for future security. Some people may not be entirely cooperative, so you may have to push a little to get at the facts you need. The number 2 is important.

Friday, August 17: You are straining against your harness today and would like to be off and running. It is frustrating to have people after you to join them in some interesting activities. Pace yourself today and soon you will have the time. The attention you devote to nitty-gritty tasks today will save you time later.

Saturday, August 18: You've got a lot of people on your side but take some steps to make sure they will stay there. Patience is needed by all—including you. Don't let their enthusiasm cool; spend the time making initial steps and clearing the path for progress. The significant number is 4.

Sunday, August 19: Now you are ready to roll, and it's no longer necessary to play it safe. You play the go-getter today with conviction and authority and you make your mark on a situation in a way that leaves no one in doubt who's in charge. No matter what else happens, there is time for a pleasant and possibly productive romantic interlude.

Monday, August 20: People are often drawn to you for your reasonable way of handling things. You are famous for being fair when it comes to looking at both sides of a question. Today your sense of justice is rewarded by a grateful person who lets you in on some inside information you can turn to profit. It pays to be a good person.

Tuesday, August 21: Nobody's perfect, and wishing won't make it so. Be sure you are looking at someone in a realistic light when you assess his or her capabilities. You can still make a vast improvement in the conditions that need changing; ask people to do what they are best at and nothing more. That includes you.

Wednesday, August 22: It pays to be the boss when somebody wants to make you decide and you are not ready to. You can simply pull rank. You do that today and it is a good idea. It gives you the time you need to clear your mind and look at things rationally. Too many wrong decisions are made in haste, and you of all people do not want to fall prey to that.

Thursday, August 23: Today you should aim high, in every sense of the word. You can afford to shoot for the moon in terms of success, but you must keep your principles just as lofty. Think in terms of everyone's rights before you take a step. It is encouraging to have the support of an enthusiastic cohort—who is possibly an Aries.

Friday, August 24: You are feeling your oats today. As you kick up your heels you find you want to express yourself differently; as you take what is for you an unorthodox approach, others are surprised—but delighted. Your partnership status benefits by your upbeat mood as well. The number for you to experiment with today is 1.

Saturday, August 25: Unlike yesterday, discretion is the order of the day. You can't afford to fool around when you are dealing with what belongs to someone else. Make sure you've got your pins all lined up before you bowl the ball—even if it means postponing a scheduled "signing."

Sunday, August 26: You are in such an expansive mood today you might take on more than you can handle. All kinds of things are brewing in your mind and a lot of big thinking is going on. Take it one step at a time. You get a real lift when a turn of events brings something you desperately want a little closer. The number to watch today is 5.

Monday, August 27: Your lust for travel is stimulated today by an encounter with someone from another country. Once again it is important not to become hyperactive and get nothing done. There is a big project that someone's got under control and wants you to play a major role in. It's the kind of job you can sink your teeth into and you do. The lucky number is 22 today.

Tuesday, August 28: That's more like it! Now you are doing some really creative thinking instead of just spinning your wheels. What gets you going is a couple of pretty fascinating people who offer a challenge. It's a friendly one, however, and does you a world of good.

Wednesday, August 29: You could be tempted to be a bit manipulative today when someone is wide open to it. Resist the urge; one of your strongest points is your reasonable approach and your understandable behavior. You are pivotal to calming down a situation that's been a bit hot; you get a round of cheers from the people involved.

Thursday, August 30: Today you are forced to play a background role, but you don't mind. You would just as soon lay back and watch the scenario. The group you observe has a common purpose, but today it seems to be temporarily lost. It doesn't appear that your taking an active role would help very much. The number 7 appears important.

Friday, August 31: Now it's time for you to get into the act. Your prestige is such that you can be very effective—and net yourself more power. By waiting for the right moment to strike you make the most of the situation and come closer to what you want.

September 1984

Astronote to Capricorn: It's amazing how the month of September brings thoughts of job-changing or career-switching. In some ways, the end of the summer is really the start of a new year. Even if you do not find yourself among the many who are scanning the help-wanted columns this month, it's a good time to look at Capricorn in terms of the sign's job style.

Obviously Capricorn is dependable. Obviously Capricorn is hard-working. No one doubts Capricorn's mental capacity, and there is general agreement that the sign is well-organized. What more do you want in an employee—or a boss, for that matter? A spark of originality and enough wit and personality to add something to the office mix. Some Capricorns can be so industrious that they make everyone else feel guilty about an occasional joke or fast repartee on a nonbusiness subject. Hence, it is sometimes difficult for Capricorn to be totally accepted by his or her peers. Even Capricorn's boss feels a little funny about taking long lunches or relaxing a bit on the job.

The message is clear: if on-the-job companionship and compatibility means anything to you (and it should), lighten up, loosen up, and dare to dillydally once in a while. The human element in job happiness and career success cannot be overemphasized. When the Capricorn reaches boss level, he or she should never forget it. The most important resource in any business office or plant is the people who work there. They are not automatons, and Capricorn should demonstrate that he or she knows it by reaching out and making warm gestures—especially when things are rough. Capricorn is so naturally industrious that it may not occur to him or her that not everyone is so willing to put in that extra effort. Not unless you sweeten the pot with a little extra warmth and consideration.

Saturday, September 1: You didn't know quite what to expect from a reunion between you and your most important person today. In spite of your apprehension, it goes very well—in fact, you are surprised at how well. It feels good to be back in synch. In another matter you've got to exercise patience because waiting is the key to winning this game. The number 6 is lucky today.

Sunday, September 2: You surprise everyone when you reveal some work you've been doing in private. Their enthusiasm for your project and the ideas that are thrown at you about how to put it to work are exciting to you and you can't wait to get on with it. It's great to have a goal and know where you are going.

151

Monday, September 3: You feel compelled toward a certain action today in a way that seems mysterious. There is something fated in what you do. You are so direct with someone that it provokes a crisis in the relationship. Now that the cards are on the table time will tell what course it will take.

Tuesday, September 4: MOON IN CAPRICORN. Now you see what the waiting was all about; it pays off now because you are prepared when an opportunity—a kind of test—is thrown at you. You pass with flying colors because you are well prepared. Listen to someone with a sense of flair when he or she brings up the subject of your image.

Wednesday, September 5: The tips you picked up yesterday give you even more charisma today; you find it's easy to express yourself quite forcefully and to turn a certain situation around. It's a good day to indulge your taste for the arts; you might even try your hand at painting and writing yourself. The number to watch is 1.

Thursday, September 6: Today is a day to take stock of resources and see where you can make a good thing even better. As you put it all together you are helped by someone close to you who has your interests at heart. She (and it is a she) offers sound advice about stretching something so it will go farther.

Friday, September 7: There's a big pull on you today; two things fight for your attention. One is your adventurous mood and the other is the need to be practical. For now, pull in your reins and let reality dominate. When you get things in better shape there will be plenty of time to experiment. A lively companion provides some comic relief.

Saturday, September 8: This is solid-citizen day where you appreciate your stable base of operations. It is comforting to you to have established routines so that everyone knows his or his part. You play yours very well by figuring out some new ways to make things safer and sounder.

Sunday, September 9: A riddle gets solved today when you apply some creative thinking to a complex situation. *You* see the light and it changes your view of things totally. The problem is that others do not get it as quickly. It's up to you to explain things in a new way that everyone can understand, and react to accordingly.

Monday, September 10: A community project gets everyone pitching in and working toward a common goal—which may be making things more attractive than they were. You personally get a lot of satisfaction out of it—not only the results but the experience of rubbing shoulders with some very nice people in the process.

Tuesday, September 11: Whenever a Pisces is involved do not expect the obvious. An individual of that sign crosses your stage today and you are left wondering what he or she was all about. Don't let your confusion divert you from the work at hand; in fact, a clue you pick up from Pisces can be very helpful in getting to the bottom of a mystery.

Wednesday, September 12: You are feeling pretty mellow today—in fact, emotionally fulfilled. Your pleasant mood moves you to see where you can be particularly helpful to others. The help you give may involve the purchase of something that makes life easier for everyone involved and you feel the expenditure is worth it.

Thursday, September 13: What you want is now, not "somewhere over the rainbow," but a real possibility. You've got to make an almost heroic effort, but you're working off a very strong base. Somebody with a lot of guts—possibly an Aries—is right there beside you. It's one of those cases where if you want something badly enough you can get it.

Friday, September 14: Today's the day you "go for it" and assert yourself. It's a little scary, but when you get

153

your new deal it will put you in on the ground floor of something big. You are doing it not only for yourself but for some other very important people—among whom may be children. The number 11 could be important.

Saturday, September 15: It bugs you that things are going so slowly and you may feel quite irritated. Don't take it out on others. You are so fanatic about being sure about things that it is difficult for you to tolerate uncertainty. Take your mind off it for now by planning an evening out with a pleasant dinner and some genial company.

Mid-month memo to Capricorn: Where does the ambitious, hard-working, logical Capricorn look for the most compatible career? Here are some possibilities based on the sign's natural talents and astrological associations:

Banking and finance, many phases, including mortgage work; middle and top management in virtually any big business or industry; all levels of government bureaucracy—state, federal, and local; dentistry; orthopedics; geriatrics; education, mainly the administrative areas; any "numbers" work, including economics, accounting, financial management; some phases of the arts, particularly sculpture; the physical sciences, particularly earth studies, such as geology; real estate and construction, all phases, including skilled and labor; lab work in both industrial and human research; correctional work, including police work, regulatory services, supervision of those needing correction.

Sunday, September 16: Things pick up a lot today and you are in a better mood. There's a lot you could choose from in the way of activity today, but you are selective. In choosing the best you demonstrate your innate preference for quality over quantity. Today, the lucky number is 3.

Monday, September 17: A lot of people want your opinion today—isn't it nice to be respected? It's a big responsibility, though, because your vote could swing a

154

big project one way or the other. In another matter, be a bit skeptical when someone tries to sell you a bill of goods. There may be some catches hidden between the lines.

Tuesday, September 18: One of your relationships has been taking a more serious turn of late; today may be the day it gets locked into place. For those without a lifetime partner this could be it. Don't forget that you've promised to keep somebody completely clued in; pick up the phone or drop a note so he or she won't feel left out.

Wednesday, September 19: You have a direct exchange of ideas or products with your "public" today. Buying and selling are the order of the day, even if it's only in terms of your own personality. You've got some responsibilities to fulfill at home, too, however, so don't linger too long with your prospects. A legal contract may need looking at.

Thursday, September 20: There's an air of deception in the scenario today, and you could be the worst deceiver. First you must look at your own views with absolute dispassion. The next step is to demand the real story from some people who try to do a cover-up. You'll probably have to investigate on your own. Lucky 7 is today's number.

Friday, September 21: You exert a powerful influence today and could get yourself a lot of points. Some may come when you go into an overtime situation which demonstrates how dedicated to the cause you are. In your mind you know you will be compensated handsomely. You do set an example for others, however, and that's not all bad.

Saturday, September 22: Some people who have backed you want to see some returns on their investment today. It may take the form of your showing how much you've learned. Be appreciative and generous with your time.

You can't lose sight of the fact that you wouldn't be where you are if they hadn't helped.

Sunday, September 23: Despite the day, you've got to go like sixty to meet a pressing deadline. The more you streamline things and improve your methods the faster it will go. You are excited because a whole new chapter is starting and you can't wait to get on with it. Someone may not share your views, however; see if your philosophy meets the challenge.

Monday, September 24: Your inclination is to be stingy as you count every penny to see where you are. It's possible to be a little looser than you are inclined to be. You may have to spring for a trip that involves relatives, and it's an area where you simply can't stint. The number 2 is good today.

Tuesday, September 25: You can afford to relax and rest on your laurels today. The pressure is off, even if only temporarily. You are so popular, you might have the tendency to be a little smug with people you'd love to impress. If you are not careful, you may get your comeuppance by losing something as you go from place to place today.

Wednesday, September 26: It's obvious you've got to be a team player today. As you reestablish ties with those you work with you are able to regroup and get organized. It's necessary to get up the steam to clear a big hurdle, and you've all got to rise above petty concerns. The common enemy may be a Scorpio.

Thursday, September 27: You are honored to be honored today by a group of people who feel you've really earned it. It gives you the perfect opportunity to self-promote—especially something you want to advertise. If you are in the mood for it, a romantic opportunity is there for the asking. Today's number is 5.

Friday, September 28: You are feeling a bit wistful today and in the mood for someone or something beau-

tiful to come your way. In preparation you dress up
and pay more attention than usual to your appearance.
It is as if you know some pleasant activities are in store.
You are not even surprised when one of your wishes
comes true through something that lands in your lap.

Saturday, September 29: Be sure to be discreet today;
you will be involved in a secret meeting that is of
considerable importance to someone else. You discipline yourself to remain silent. In fact, you retire al-
together and use the time for private meditation.

Sunday, September 30: You are on the brink of signing
an important contract. Don't take it for granted until
it's in the bag. You know you've made the right decision and you don't want to take any chances. Keep an
eye out for another Capricorn who may be involved.
The number to watch is 8.

October 1984

Astronote to Capricorn: There is a closed system in
astrology which associates each of the zodiacal signs with
one of the planets. These planetary assignments are
based on ancient tradition and are very revealing in terms
of the "why" of each sign's particular characteristics.

Capricorn has from earliest ages been connected with
the planet Saturn. Saturn rules Capricorn with an iron
hand, which is Saturn's style—and hence Capricorn's.
Saturn has been known by other names in other times,
but all of them involve time, age, and responsibility.
For instance, once Saturn was Kronos, whose sin was
usurping his father's throne among the gods and eating all his children so they would not compete with
him. Zeus survived, however, and wreaked terrible re-
venge on Kronos. He was exiled forever and forced to
wander as the creaky, decrepit figure we characterize
as "Father Time." The connection between the name
Kronos and our word "chronology" is fairly obvious.
Saturn does mark off the inevitable aging process that

takes place with time. He also stands guard over man's tendency to excess; when we get too carried away, Saturn comes along and reminds us that there are limits. Saturn's benefits balance out the heavy planet's detriments, however, and in that respect it is aptly assigned to Capricorn. Responsibility, sense of purpose, and devotion to duty may not be considered among the more personable of virtues—but they generally make for a good human being.

Monday, October 1: MOON IN CAPRICORN. Someone's putting the pressure on to bust loose—and it may be you. You are driven toward perfection, and the way you realign things shows just how skillful you are. When the kudos come for your performance, you are not surprised, because you were confident you knew what you were doing. Don't get a swelled head.

Tuesday, October 2: You are thinking very big these days, and piddling matters are of no concern to you. You are anxious to play the leader so that you will get a following. You do, but not without cost to you. So bear in mind that today's lucky number is 8.

Wednesday, October 3: You of all people cannot tolerate the tawdry or shoddy, and it's necessary for you to do some clearing of the decks today to eliminate what you do not want. Others may be a bit shocked at your actions, but they should know that you want nothing but quality and will insist on having it. An impulsive Aries may be rather annoyed.

Thursday, October 4: What you did yesterday has had a contagious effect on those around you. Suddenly you and everyone else get a lot smarter about how to manage time, tools, and resources. The harmony is great for productivity. The number 1 is lucky for you.

Friday, October 5: Back off a bit today; you've been going at it pretty heavily and need some rest and recuperation time. If you are tuned in to your own "mechanics" you will see that you need some refueling now.

Just being alone and quiet in your own little place is the wise decision. Today number 2 is the lucky one for you.

Saturday, October 6: Time to resurface from your private world and get back into the action. The respite gave you back your perspective—and your sense of humor. It gets put to work today when others seem to be floored by too much to do. You, however, polish off your work in no time and cheerfully, too. You've got time to play in the bargain.

Sunday, October 7: This is a day of rather mixed emotions. You are a bit annoyed when someone puts you to the test, but you do well when you demonstrate you are able to revise a scheme according to new input. A light touch is provided by a pal or relative who drops in and makes everybody loosen up and laugh a bit. The respite possibly comes from a Sagittarian.

Monday, October 8: Today there is an undercurrent of seriousness, though on the surface you seem quite care-free and amused by some entertainment someone provides. However, you are really thinking about how relieved you are that an estrangement is rapidly healing and you are drawing close to someone you felt terrible about being on the outs with.

Tuesday, October 9: Home is where your heart is today, no matter where you are. There are a lot of good feelings generated by some mutual projects that have helped everyone involved feel creative. A difficult incident seems far behind and there is a general sharing of affection. Your lucky number is 6.

Wednesday, October 10: Today you need to get away from it all—home, work, the whole kit. Your privacy is very important because it gives you a chance to breathe deeply and get your priorities back in order. As you commune with nature, you've got to face the fact that a certain chapter in your life is rapidly coming to a close.

Thursday, October 11: You get some great tips from a fellow Capricorn and they teach you such a lesson you can't wait to put it to work. The theory tests out well in practice, and you get a real kick out of your discovery. Nice going!

Friday, October 12: Today you convey a plan of action to the higher-ups, and you yourself aim high. You are frustrated with certain limitations and are aching to go beyond them. You are in a good position to sell yourself and your talents, and a Libran comes to the fore with help and support.

Saturday, October 13: The points you scored yesterday put you in a celebrating mood today. You feel like kicking up your heels and doing something *you* want to do. Indulging in a personal taste in entertainment gives you special pleasure—even more so because a romantic partner enjoys it along with you. Once again number 1 is your lucky one.

Sunday, October 14: There's a big item up on the selling block today and you are on one side of the transaction or the other. Either way, don't commit yourself to anything until you get an expert's advice on the true value. Also, get together with your partner and look at all the options in a realistic manner.

Monday, October 15: Speaking of options, today you seem to have so many that it's mind-boggling. Let a friendly person—possibly a Sagittarian—untangle the mess of possibilities for you so they will be clearer to see. It's one time even *you* need an advisor in an area that appears to be financial.

Mid-month memo to Capricorn: Among the less pleasant things associated with Saturn is melancholy. In the Middle Ages, depressives were judged as having too much of the humor "black bile," and it was associated with the heavy planet Saturn. Everything about Saturn is weighty—the natural resources connected with it are rock, granite, and lead. You don't have to use too much imagination to visualize the saturnine depressive who suffers under such a heavy load. It is imperative that the Capricorn stay alert to early warnings of depression, which is not only a real illness but a potentially crippling one as well. Other astrological elements in a particular Capricorn's horoscope can provide an effective counterbalance to Saturn's woes, but in general Capricorn's tendency to take everything seriously can become excessive.

Tuesday, October 16: It may pain you a little to pass up an interesting invitation, but home and family commitments make it impossible for you to accept. You take the matter philosophically and do what needs to be done without complaining. The spirit of cooperation that reigns is marvelous to behold. The harmony goes beyond personal partnerships and includes professional ones.

Wednesday, October 17: Prompt action is crucial to a legal matter today. There's no time to waste in getting the proper information to the right people. It may be you who is awaiting something that will clarify a situation for you. Don't panic. Call on a helpful friend who understands tricky business like this. You are not subtle enough. Test number 5 for luck.

Thursday, October 18: The emotional climate in your home surroundings changes dramatically for the better now. There is almost a spirit of celebration, and someone gives someone a lavish gift—possibly connected with music. The reason for celebration is a windfall that benefits everyone.

Friday, October 19: It's good to get free of a commitment that's been holding you back. Once you get clear you are able to look ahead and start to put together a travel plan. The people you plan with may have some very different ideas from your own about what constitutes a great trip.

Saturday, October 20: Perhaps in connection with your travel talk of yesterday, today you are involved with someone of another culture. It is an intriguing diversion, but you must get back to the work at hand, which involves some critical decisions you have to make. The subject is money and possibly a lot of it. A powerful person may pit his or her will against yours.

Sunday, October 21: Some things that went on yesterday struck you as quite petty. Today you resolve to rise above such attitudes and take a much broader view. Your thoughts are so lofty that you want to shut out any ugliness, so you may be inclined to spend a great part of the day in solitude. Number 9 could be lucky for you.

Monday, October 22: You bounce back today with so much vim and vigor that friends comment on the new you. You know it's partly a result of yesterday's meditation. You become aware that although you are in a period of transition, you are on your way to better things. The support and approval you get tell you so.

Tuesday, October 23: You know where you stand and it's in a pretty good place; your prestige is very much on your mind. So much so that you decide you can't waste time on anything that is not absolutely in line with the main issue. You'll catch up with pleasure pursuits later on. A partner may be disappointed.

Wednesday, October 24: A bit of the pressure is off for now so you can relax and enjoy some social activity—and suddenly there seems to be a lot of it. Pick and choose carefully so you don't overdo; you are usually sensible enough to know when to stop.

Thursday, October 25: You wake with a clear mind that is ready to deal with all kinds of practical and even technical matters. Others praise you when you get the rules down pat the first time around. However, all is not as sweet as it seems; read between the lines to pick up some possibly unfriendly vibes. And look to number 4 for luck.

Friday, October 26: The pace slows down today, giving you a chance to look around at those closest to you. Their love and support is very meaningful to you and you resolve to be more sensitive to their needs. In fact, you feel quite romantic and in the mood for an intimate chat. Get away with that special someone and let others handle the chores.

Saturday, October 27: You want to stick close to home today and really wish everybody else would stay away. There are some excellent emotional vibes around you and you want to enjoy them. You've just finished a big job and that's brought you a sense of security in the financial area. Now you want the other kind.

Sunday, October 28: A pensive mood and an inclination to look beyond the here and now lead you to some amazing insights today. They are not the kind you can easily communicate to others, but there is one—possibly a Pisces—who understands. You find you are no longer uneasy about what you used to call mysterious.

Monday, October 29: MOON IN CAPRICORN. It's as if you were shot out of a cannon today. The very power of your will and personality bring about changes even you are surprised at. Don't be afraid to let go of the status quo. Jump into the driver's seat with confidence. Your only possible hazard is attempting to do too much too quickly. Your lucky number is 8.

Tuesday, October 30: Now you've got a reputation for meaning business. Don't let it precede you and intimidate others, however. You can get cooperation out of others without browbeating them—particularly an Aries who is dying to get in on the act. Encouraging others to participate more will strengthen relationships.

Wednesday, October 31: You've been getting quite a few chances to show your style lately. Today another opportunity comes along and you act independently in such a cool and confident manner that it impresses a

163

lot of people. Don't sit and preen your feathers, however; get to the heart of something important. You may also run right into romance. And the number 1 could bring you good luck.

November 1984

Astronote to Capricorn: According to the ancient "law of correspondences," the heavens above are an accurate reflection of the world below, and there are innumerable one-to-one connections. The people, places, and things influenced by Capricorn and its ruling planet Saturn may also be influenced by subjects naturally associated with the sign and the planet. Such subjects, for example, as:

Abandoned places; beasts of burden; archeology; aged persons; conservation; censors; calendars; causes; customs; economics; gates; gravel; ice dealers; hibernation; poison ivy; monasteries; mountain climbers; natural resources; night watchmen; potters; slaves; sedatives; Satan; solitaire; surveyors; underground vaults; wallets; wealth; widowers; Greece; Lithuania; jails; contractors; Siberia; pyramids; sextons; black poppies; fallow ground; cryogenics; dark colors; Jack Frost; Albania; common sense; delays; endurance; history.

Thursday, November 1: You can make a power play today—though you may go about it in a rather quiet manner. The tack you should take is to gather all the material and organize it in a way that supports your case so that no one has any doubt. This kind of rational approach will favorably impress some people who can do a lot for your cause.

Friday, November 2: Do not concern yourself with what is petty or insignificant today; you've got too much big thinking to do. There are those who would break your concentration and waste your time; let them know you are out of touch for the day. Some family members do need a piece of you, however, and what they ask for is legitimate.

Saturday, November 3: Yesterday's philosophizing has given you new perspective, and that in turn spurs you on to a new way of acting. It is well-focused action, because you have the courage of your convictions. In fact, you have your objectives so well outlined you've put them on paper! Relatives can be more helpful than you think in your new endeavor. The lucky number is 1.

Sunday, November 4: Regardless of your sex, you may have a touch of woman's intuition today; the inspiration comes from an older female who is very wise in matters of the heart such as this. Trust her. You are too emotional today to allow logic to control; never fear—it will come back strong. Keep the social activity at a minimum, however, because you could become overstimulated.

Monday, November 5: You've got a special spark today and it manifests itself in a delightful sense of humor. In your light manner, you manage to express yourself very clearly and get your point across. A deal is consummated in your favor and it may involve real estate. You are sympatico with a Sagittarian.

Tuesday, November 6: Don't let your enthusiasm run down to the point where you leave something half done. Persist and do not compromise. Your outlook makes a lot of sense to a lot of people—some of whom are willing to back you. There's solid ground under your feet. Today's power number is 22.

Wednesday, November 7: Someone you love delights and surprises you today with a message that says he or she loves you in a very special way. The mood of the day tends to pleasure and entertainment, and you may enjoy yourself even more if children are part of the scenario.

Thursday, November 8: You get a warm feeling again today when someone proves his or her affection. There's no doubt about it now! It makes you feel so good you make a special effort to look the part and make your surroundings harmonize as well. Someone piques your curiosity by telling you of a risky venture. You determine to learn more.

Friday, November 9: Try to stay out of the spotlight today because it may tend to distract you. What you need to do is best done on your own and away from others. One person appeals for some special time with you, and you oblige, because he or she senses your mood and reacts to it. He or she is also a little mysterious about what it's all about.

Saturday, November 10: You feel like a "fat cat" today when an old, almost forgotten debt is repaid. And you find a pleasanter environment after you play peacemaker and get everyone to go along with the plan. Speaking of fat cats, you also decide your diet needs some attention.

Sunday, November 11: You hit upon something today that touches a familiar note in everyone involved. Suddenly your concept is evoking a lot of interest and you are able to express it with more confidence. Maybe you really have something here! Pursue it along with a rather adventurous type who's a little more willing to experiment with you. Get lucky with number 9.

Monday, November 12: You start the day in high gear and stay that way throughout. Yesterday's experience gives you the confidence to open up and say some things that are on your mind. Others find it challenging, but do not fight you on it. You did well to trust your intuition that you would find a receptive attitude and a willingness to form a partnership.

Tuesday, November 13: Today you lay back and let the others do the talking; you learn a lot more by observing and listening. Some important negotiations command your attention, but a bell goes off in your head about some catching up you have to do with payments that are falling due. Don't fall behind.

Wednesday, November 14: It's important to focus in on personal financial matters, so you decide to devote some time and effort to them. It is amazing what you are able to accomplish. You get some details of an agreement worked out and find it actually increases your cash flow. Nice going! Now you can concentrate on a visit you want to make.

Thursday, November 15: You are wise to be particularly cautious now and not speculate about something that is not certain. If you are really interested, why not do some homework and see what the potential is? Don't be embarrassed to ask a clued-in friend to help; he or she won't tell anyone.

Mid-month memo to Capricorn: From ancient times there have been acknowledged connections between each sign or planet and parts of the human body, as well as their illnesses. Here's what the medical astrologer lists under the "rulership" of Saturn/Capricorn:

Chronic ailments of all kinds; the bones in general; the joints; the knees; skin blemishes; colds; congestion; constipation; the teeth; tooth decay; gall bladder and gall stones; the gonads; hives; hyperacidity; depression; paralysis; itching; the ligaments; lupus; arthritis; disease prevention; psoriasis; the skin in general; retardation; rheumatism; transplants; pruritis.

Friday, November 16: At first you pull a blank when someone tries to remind you of an old incident; then you remember and have a good laugh over it. The sense of camaraderie goes a long way toward helping your public relations in the situation. Nothing brings people together like talking over old times. Luck out with number 5.

Saturday, November 17: A small purchase makes a big hit with the family, and it paves the way for your telling everyone you need a place to retreat to. You manage to find a small spot where you can do some quiet reading and studying. Everyone regards the arrangement as an improvement.

Sunday, November 18: You are way out there again today as your mind travels while your body stays at home. You enjoy the vicarious journey because it opens up a whole new world for you. Suddenly you are impatient with anything phony or artificial; a close friend agrees with your point of view.

Monday, November 19: You run smack into a public situation today in which you are virtually on display. Fortunately you enjoy being able to flex your muscles and show your power. You may find yourself competing with another determined person—possibly a fellow Capricorn. Remember some precedents you have set and don't fight dirty.

Tuesday, November 20: New prestige and a feeling that others are giving you high marks make it easy to forget past mistakes now. With a few successes under your belt you are finally beginning to get some confidence that you can continue to perform well. Don't lose the feeling! And don't overlook lucky number 9.

Wednesday, November 21: Breaking ties with past people and outworn habits is not always easy, but with the burst of energy and confidence you feel now, you are able to do it. As a result, you open doors to new opportunities—and even romance. Your activities today revolve around a group dedicated to a worthy cause and you enjoy the involvement. A wish is close to coming true.

Thursday, November 22: You hope it is not a wild goose chase you set out on today; nobody seems to have the straight story and it's up to you to get it. There is even a hint of mystery and a slight apprehension about what is involved. When you see the light,

168

you get a good laugh. It's amazing what your imagination can do.

Friday, November 23: Nobody loves a party more than you—that is, when you are comfortable with the company. Your shyness might be strained more than you like by a gathering you are invited to today, however. Skip it, and join a hearty Sagittarian who challenges you to a round of tennis or other outdoor sport. Don't overdo, though.

Saturday, November 24: You bounce back from yesterday's strenuous activities and are ready to attack a big project. You've got to tear something apart before you can build it up again, but you are up to the challenge. Once you get a few roadblocks out of the way—and get a flash about how to cut corners—the whole thing goes easily. The lucky number is 4.

Sunday, November 25: MOON IN CAPRICORN. You have a lot of loyal supporters today—particularly a member of the opposite sex who may have an ulterior motive. He or she is harmless, however, so you shouldn't hesitate to join in a proposed adventure. Something you put on paper recently is very well received and nets you the vote of an influential person.

Monday, November 26: Work around the house, whatever its nature, is fun and games to you today. Your flexible and upbeat attitude shows the change that's come over you through some recent successes. Whatever you do today you want to do well and you enjoy instructing some novices in the right way to do things.

Tuesday, November 27: You've been around people a lot the past few days, so today you find it a relief to have some privacy. You do need time to think now—especially about how to preserve your new good feelings about yourself. One way is to define what's really important to you and then make a long-range plan about how to go after it. You've got all the time in the world. Number 7 likes you today.

Wednesday, November 28: You have decided to take things one step at a time and today you take a small one that is nevertheless important. The commitment you make is based on facts, not fantasy. You are sure that the rewards will be solid when they come. Do some stock-taking around the house in line with your plan to get organized.

Thursday, November 29: There's some funny stuff going on and you may get caught right in the middle. Try to take a mature attitude even if others don't. If you are dragged into it, don't take sides; just let each person know that there is something to value in everyone. You may be surprised how influential you can be in helping others see the light.

Friday, November 30: You've got a lot of steam today and accept with enthusiasm when you are asked to join in an outing with friends or neighbors. It does a lot for your morale; you also get to know some people worth knowing. One person in particular is drawn to you, and you feel the same. It looks like the beginning of a good friendship. The lucky number is 1.

December 1984

Astronote to Capricorn: It's always fun to look at the famous and the infamous born under your sign and see if they have any similar characteristics or talents. This mixed bag of people were born under the sign of Capricorn:

Steve Allen; Humphrey Bogart; Pablo Casals; Nat "King" Cole; Barry Goldwater; J. Edgar Hoover; Howard Hughes; Martin Luther King, Jr.; Richard Nixon; Horatio Alger; Al Capone; Marlene Dietrich; Danny Kaye; Ethel Merman; Dolly Parton; Elvis Presley; Anwar Sadat; Joseph Stalin; Ava Gardner; Mao Tse-tung; Carl Sandburg; Muhammad Ali; Joan Baez; Cary Grant; Mary Tyler Moore; Gypsy Rose Lee; David Bowie; Paul Cézanne.

Saturday, December 1: Today you stumble upon something very enlightening; there was a lesson waiting to be learned right under your nose. It may come about as you do some household inventory and try to assess how much some things are worth. It may be the motives of others you are weighing, too. You've got to think of yourself first—but close relatives need consideration, too.

Sunday, December 2: Today you find you have to throw your weight around to impress upon the family the necessity of being more careful and conservative. Don't play the heavy, however; if you make it clear that it's all in the best interests of everyone, you'll get the cooperation you need. An old pal says, "My, how you've changed."

Monday, December 3: Inspiration guides you and you can see a small ray of hope that a long-held dream can come true. Your extreme sensitivity makes this vision quite clear and you understand you are operating out of basically altruistic motives. Don't shortchange yourself in the process, however. Consult with a clearheaded friend, who will set you straight.

Tuesday, December 4: You are able to play the expert today and fill in others on what you've learned through your investigation. It makes you feel good. Be sure to handle things with a light touch, however, or you will dampen the party atmosphere at the gathering. A travel tip comes by phone. Try your luck with number 3.

Wednesday, December 5: Sometimes you are known as "old reliable"; don't spoil your reputation by neglecting to keep a commitment you made recently. A sibling relationship gets a nice boost when you find yourself planning together for a joint venture. Be sure to define terms absolutely clearly; it is most important when dealing with family.

Thursday, December 6: You are bursting with ideas today, but they will come to naught unless you figure

171

out ways to put them to work for you. Advertise yourself! When you want to you can be very entertaining, and a light touch is the clue today. You are a bit distracted by a little mystery that intrigues you. Number 5 could have a bearing on good news.

Friday, December 7: Today you feel like luxuriating in the peaceful and pleasant atmosphere of your own home. People are being especially nice to each other, and it's great to have harmony all around. You celebrate it with a gift—possibly flowers. A pleasure-loving Taurus may be enjoying the atmosphere with you.

Saturday, December 8: Someone may try to weasel something out of you today—it could be money or information. Keep your eyes wide open and be alert when someone tries to pull the wool over them. He or she is so interested in what you are interested in that it's hard to resist the overture. If you go along, be sure to read the fine print.

Sunday, December 9: You are in a great spot to negotiate today; in fact, yours is the power position. Use it to get the terms you want in a deal that's near closing and could involve a change of residence. The person you negotiate with is no match for you in terms of mental acumen.

Monday, December 10: Stick to the tried-and-true today, even if it's a bit of a bore. This is not the time to try any new tricks or begin another project. Think of it as clearing your mental slate, so you will be ready for some challenging things that will soon come along. Keep lucky number 9 in mind.

Tuesday, December 11: Someone says "Go!" and you rush to center stage with your innovative idea. You were wise to wait until the coast was clear. However, there's someone who isn't at all sure about this new plan. You are going to have to push a little; however, you will get farther by turning on the charm and trying a public relations approach.

172

Wednesday, December 12: You get a bit of shock today when something comes out of the blue and causes a quick turnaround of a familiar situation. It impresses you deeply and brings up some deep-down memories of events and people from your past. The best thing is to assimilate the new input and let it sit for a few days before you decide to act.

Thursday, December 13: It's kind of fun to pull a surprise on someone who does not expect it. You get a big kick out of pulling it off—especially after the first hubbub calms down. The mood you are in goes a long way in relieving your mind of something that's been weighing you down. A Sagittarian may offer some sage advice.

Friday, December 14: You are thinking on the grand scale today, and the possibilities of new adventure excite you. There's something you've got to set to rights before it can become a reality, but you are willing to put in the time and effort. Someone inspires you and makes you feel a lot better about a secret fear you have.

Saturday, December 15: Don't jump at something that looks like a bargain today; you'll have to examine it closely first for some possible flaws. Restrain yourself and analyze things before you act. Someone with a good mind for such things is a big help; it is possibly a Virgo who has had experience with these things in the past.

Mid-month memo to Capricorn: There are a couple of themes that seem to run through the list of famous Capricorns, and one is the unusual number of "heavies"— from Mao Tse-tung to Al Capone to J. Edgar Hoover to Richard M. Nixon. Good or bad, none of the above could be called your carefree, happy-go-lucky type. Longevity also seems to bless the famous Capricorn; Pablo Casals was not only alive but active in music well into his nineties, and Marlene Dietrich shows no signs of giving up. Some obvious "depressives"—at least not just garden-variety neurotics—are Elvis Presley and Howard Hughes.

Sunday, December 16: Nothing angers you more than someone who doesn't play fair. You spot someone at it today and you decide to outwit him or her. You can do it and stay within the rules if you are clever. The team that supports you wants very much for you to win; the support gives you a warm feeling about your partner.

Monday, December 17: Something doesn't seem quite right to you; when you ask for details you see that you've been in the dark about what is really going on. You have to go through the back door to get the facts, but you have every right to in this situation. You will get an acknowledgment of your good judgment in due time.

Tuesday, December 18: You are one to organize things today when you assume leadership of a group that's a bit confused. Everyone knows they can depend on you to set things to rights. Your performance is so good the experience becomes a profitable one for you—particularly in terms of psychic income. The number to trust today is 8.

Wednesday, December 19: You made such an impressive showing yesterday that everybody's after you for your advice and counsel today. You like having a forum for your ideas. In one area you are able to get across and win on a major point that's been a sticking point for some time. In the course of it you go head-to-head with a rather abrasive individual.

Thursday, December 20: The minute you find out some new factors that are the clue to what has been a murky situation, you should take action. In this case you are not jumping the gun and you will score big with some people who prove less decisive than you. You enjoy the recognition.

Friday, December 21: Your "sixth sense" tells you something big is brewing and you get your responses ready. Since you are smart enough to prepare yourself you've got the jump on everyone else. Smart move! Now that you've got the go-ahead, take care not to take any unnecessary risks. A tuned-in buddy—possibly a Pisces—can help a lot in this regard.

Saturday, December 22: MOON IN CAPRICORN. What a great day to dress up and step out into the spotlight. You've got that "can't fail" feeling and you feel ready for anything. Something unexpected does occur which makes you have to hustle, but you do it so well you impress everyone—particularly a member of the opposite sex.

Sunday, December 23: Everyone else seems to be running around in circles, so you decide to grab the reins. It's simple for you to spot the problem and get everybody to regroup in a more productive way. Your restructuring is obviously the key to success in this enterprise and you enjoy a moment of glory. Today's lucky number, 4, may have something to do with it.

Monday, December 24: A mighty important person comes into your life today. When you are introduced you get back some good vibes that match your own. He or she may be the bearer of some material you've been wanting to flesh out some of your plans. You work on it together and you make a great team.

Tuesday, December 25: This is a good holiday for you; recently you've been thinking about what's important and have your priorities in pretty good order now. It is a pleasurable family day and the accent is on reunion and reconciliation. Your lucky number is 6.

Wednesday, December 26: Warm feelings still prevail in the aftermath of the holiday and you are able to clear up an unfortunate understanding in a quiet talk. You will have to be a bit discreet about another situation in which you have a chance encounter. Someone who is not too mobile these days could be helpful in a financial situation if you contact him or her.

Thursday, December 27: You are so industrious today you almost can't stand yourself. The virtuous feeling gets stronger when you find that you are held up as an example to others; it is amost embarrassing. A romance that is blossoming is very much on your mind. As you work so diligently, others do not know you are thinking intimate thoughts.

Friday, December 28: It's important to kick yourself into taking the initiative; no one is going to do it for you. Something is so close you can almost taste it, but you'll never make the final capture unless you broadcast your cause to others. Take some tips from a very verbal friend who knows the ropes when it comes to sweet-talking the way to what you want.

Saturday, December 29: Now you've got the idea and you go into your act. The original way you project yourself is impressive and you find that people buy your ideas. See—you can create your own style if you try. A relationship is reaching a challenging point and you will have to deal with it. Number 1 is the lucky one.

Sunday, December 30: You are able to close the book on a situation today, but you have mixed emotions about it. Ending something is always a bit scary, but you have learned a lot and can consider yourself a master of the subject. Don't spread yourself too thin today by trying to please everyone. Keep your responsibilities on the home front at the top of your mind.

Monday, December 31: You feel like reaching out to others today but you may take on more than you can handle. Keep your sense of humor. You make a discovery about someone else that raises your opinion of him or her. The holiday will be a quiet one, but the family will feel close together and enjoy a feeling of mutual well-being.

ABOUT THE AUTHOR

Born on August 5, 1926, in Philadelphia, Omarr was the only astrologer ever given full-time duty in the U.S. Army as an astrologer. He also is regarded as the most erudite astrologer of our time and the best-known, through his syndicated column (300 newspapers), and his radio and television programs (he is Merv Griffin's "resident astrologer"). Omarr has been called the most "knowledgeable astrologer since Evangeline Adams." His forecasts of Nixon's downfall, the end of World War II in mid-August of 1945, the assassination of John F. Kennedy, Roosevelt's election to a fourth term and his death in office . . . these and many others . . . are on record and quoted enough to be considered "legendary."

ABOUT THIS SERIES

This is one of a series of
Twelve Day-by-Day Astrological Guides
for the signs in 1984
by Sydney Omarr

Win A Free Gift! Fill out this questionnaire and mail it today. All entries must be received by September 30, 1983. A drawing will be held in the New American Library offices in New York City on December 15, 1983. 500 winners will be randomly selected and sent a gift.

1. What is your overall opinion of this 1984 Sydney Omarr Astrology Guide? Please circle one number from 0-10 on the scale below.

    (Poor) 0 1 2 3 4 5 6 7 8 9 10 (Excellent) *(12)*

2. In total about how many popular astrology paperback guides have you purchased in the past 12 months? _____ *(14)*

3. Beside Sydney Omarr, what additional astrology guides have you purchased for yourself in the past 12 months? How would you rate them on the poor (0) to excellent (10) scale?

Title/Author	Publisher	0-10 Rating
A. _____ *(16)*	_____ *(18)*	___ *(20)*
B. _____ *(22)*	_____ *(24)*	___ *(26)*
C. _____ *(28)*	_____ *(30)*	___ *(32)*

4. What topics would you like Sidney Omarr to write about in the 1985 Astrology Guide? Please place one rating from 0-10 in the spaces provided.

    (Of least interest) 0 1 2 3 4 5 6 7 8 9 10 (Of most interest)

Topic	0-10 Rating	Topic	0-10 Rating	Topic	0-10 Rating
Love	___ *(34)*	Children	___ *(40)*	Health	___ *(46)*
Marriage	___ *(36)*	Business/Career	___ *(42)*	Travel	___ *(48)*
Family	___ *(38)*	Personal Finances	___ *(44)*	Other:	___ *(50)*

(Please Specify) *(52)*

5. What is your:

Age (54) _____

Sex (56)
Male ( )1
Female ( )2

Education (58)
High School ( )1
2 yrs college ( )2
4 yrs college ( )3
Post grad ( )4

Marital status (60)
Single ( )1
Married ( )2
Divorced ( )3
Separated ( )4
Widowed ( )5

(Please Print)

6. Name:_____

Address:_____

City:_____ State_____ Zip_____

Phone: ( )_____

(62)

Please mail to: NEW AMERICAN LIBRARY
Research Dept
1633 Broadway
New York, N.Y. 10019

Offer void where prohibited by law.

SIGNET Books of Special Interest

How your Personal Horoscope can bring you wealth, love, success and happiness.

By Norman P. Kennedy

Did you know that you can have your personal natal horoscope cast and analyzed free? You can. The American Astrological Association, the largest known astrological society in the world, is conducting astrological research. They need birth information for this project. If you send them your birth data, they'll cast your horoscope on their computer, for research purposes. And, if you wish, they'll send you a copy of it.

Your personal natal horoscope will consist of 9 pages and 3,000 words. Your horoscope will analyze your strengths and weaknesses. It will tell you how to take fuller advantage of your talents, and show you how to overcome your weaknesses. Your horoscope will discuss your lovelife, tell you who you should be sexually compatible with, and outline your marriage potentials. It will also cover your marital and child relationships along with your health, your career opportunities, and finances.

Your personal computer horoscope will not be the general kind found in paperbacks. Your horoscope will analyze your sun-sign, moon-sign, rising-sign and planets according to your exact time, date, month, year and place of birth. Many people don't understand the importance of their moon-sign and rising-sign. Your moon-sign refers to your subconscious mind relating to your past. It also affects your childhood conditioning, instinctive patterns, feelings, and inner nature. Your rising-sign shows you how to project yourself. It is the mask you wear before others.

Your horoscope will be cast on the Association's gigantic 370—145 IBM computer. It contains over 24,000,000 bits of authenticated astrological information. No two horoscopes, produced by the computer, are ever alike.

Few people realize that the majority of famous people used horoscopes just like the ones produced by the Association to discover and cultivate their talents and thus gain success and riches. Nearly all successful people use astrologers — politicians, movie stars, businessmen, doctors and lawyers. Many famous scientists were astrologers themselves; such as Sir Isaac Newton, Carl Jung and Sigmund Freud. Famous business tycoon, J.P. Morgan, used astrology to achieve his wealth. He did not make a financial move without consulting his astrologer. Astrology helped the allies win World War II by predicting the enemy's moves. A horoscope of Adolph Hitler done on January 30, 1933, exactly predicted the course of World War II. Astrology was used to find and keep the successful marriage of Grace Kelly and Prince Rainier.

These rich and famous people are no different than you and me, except for one thing. They weren't forced to use the general astrology carried in paperbacks. They could afford to pay a professional astrologer hundreds of dollars to cast their horoscope from their exact time and place of birth. Now you too can have your personal natal horoscope cast from your exact time and place of birth.

Here's how it works. The A.A.A. will cast and analyze your natal horoscope. Since your horoscope has already been produced for research, you may get it for only a $3.00 charge plus 50¢ to cover postage, handling and the cost of making your duplicate copy. You get the expensive casting and analyzing process, which could cost $250, FREE.

If you would like to help us with our research and take advantage of this special offer by ordering natal horoscopes for yourself, for your family or for your friends, simply do this: Send me the name, address, time, month, day, year and place of birth for each person on a piece of paper along with the $3.00 copying cost and 50¢ postage in cash, check or money order for each horoscope. Make checks payable to American Astrological Association. (If you don't know your exact time of birth, we'll use 12:00 noon.) If you have Master Charge or VISA, you may charge your purchase by sending the following information: A. name of your card B. credit card number C. card expiration date.

Mail your orders to the AMERICAN ASTROLOGICAL ASSOCIATION, Research Division, Dept. HH-71, 401 North Market Ave., Canton, Ohio 44750.

Your natal horoscope is covered by a one year — 365 day — full money back guarantee. To avoid a disappointment, why not order your horoscope right now, before you forget. Thanks.